THE SHIPYARD

THE SHIPYARD

◆

WILL IT FLOAT?

by Dave Drummond

iUniverse, Inc.
New York Lincoln Shanghai

THE SHIPYARD
WILL IT FLOAT?

iUniverse, Inc.

For information address:
iUniverse, Inc.
2021 Pine Lake Road, Suite 100
Lincoln, NE 68512
www.iuniverse.com

ISBN: 0-595-27532-X

Printed in the United States of America

This book is dedicated to my beloved wife, Helene. Without her encouragement and support, this book would never have been completed.

Contents

NOTABLE FIRSTS AT QUINCY

1902 seven masted schooner   The *Thomas W. Lawson* was the first and only seven masted schooner ever built.

1904 foreign submarine   First submarines built for a foreign government: six subs built for Japan.

1914 foreign battleship   The *Rivadavia* was the first battleship built in the United States for a foreign government.

1916 L Class submarines   Six L class subs; eight O class subs; 14 R class subs;
1918 O Class submarines   first mass production of submarines for the United
1919 R Class submarines   States government.

1915 H Class submarines   Twelve H class subs; first mass production of submarines for a foreign government, the British Navy.

WWI destroyers   Most destroyers built by any yard during WWI: 71 ships. Most destroyers ever built in a twenty-five month period: 71 ships. In all, more than the total output of all other United States shipyards combined.

WWII LST (landing ship tank)   Five LSTs were delivered in one fifty hour span. 326 feet long

1961 nuclear powered warship   First nuclear powered surface warship, the heavy cruiser, *Long Beach*, was delivered.

1961 heaviest ship   The world's heaviest ship, the 106,500 ton tanker, *Manhattan*, was delivered.

1962	nuclear powered destroyer	First nuclear powered destroyer, the *Bainbridge*, was delivered.
1972	Sea-bee ships	World's first sea-bee ships (barge carriers) were delivered. These had the largest elevator ever installed on any ship, including aircraft carriers. This elevator could pick up two fully loaded barges at once.
1977	LNGs	First and most successful ever built in the United States.
1983	Collier	First collier built in the United States in 40 years, this coal-carrying ship was fully automated.
1985	MPS (maritime Prepositioning Ship)	First MPS built for the United States government. Six ships delivered.

THE SHIPYARD

Growing Up

I first remember the shipyard as a boy of ten. It was always a noisy, busy, and fascinating place.

My father worked at the shipyard during World War II. At the end of the war, we moved to Quincy, one block away from the yard. My father had bought a two story house with a variety store in front. The shipyard workers came in and bought cigarettes, soda, papers, and chewing tobacco. They always looked dirty and cold or hot, depending on the season, but always dirty.

We used to play softball in a field adjacent to the yard. We could hear loud engine noises, banging, hissing, crashing, whistles, etc., and could see huge cranes swinging steel, anchors, and other items onto the ships.

When the shipyard had a launching, my friends and I would skip school. We would "borrow" a rowboat and motor down the river to watch this great event. The launching of the ocean liner _Constitution_ was an event that I had been looking forward to for a long time. When the big day arrived, my friends and I spotted a rowboat. We attached my 7 1/2 HP Firestone outboard motor and piled in. The motor was started and off we went with high hopes. One hundred feet from shore, the back fell off the boat. Luckily, the motor had been tied on. We all went swimming with our clothes on and pulled the boat back to shore.

We had a hard time finding another boat to "borrow", but finally found another skiff at a nearby dock. My friends and I went back to the scene of our earlier mishap and there stood a giant of a lobsterman with his equally huge son. They were storming around in a rage and asked us if we knew anything about their skiff with the missing stern. We told them we had seen a group of small boys in it an hour before and had chased them away. This was true, but we had chased them away so we could borrow the boat. If the lobsterman and his son had arrived fifteen minutes earlier, I might not be writing this now.

By then, we were beginning to think maybe we should have gone to school. On second thought, this was the launching of the year and there was no way we were going to miss it. The luxury liner _Constitution_ along with her sister ship, the _Independence_ were two of the most graceful ships to ever go down the ways at this historic yard. We just had to see the launching!

Arriving at the yard twenty minutes before the appointed time, we tied up a good distance from the launching ways. After all the great speeches, at exactly the right minute, the shipyard blew its raucous whistle, the tugboats tooted, and the mighty liner blew her deep throated horn. Within seconds, we could see the mighty liner start to move and ever so slowly pick up speed as she slid down the greased ways to her baptism in the water. The stern went lower and lower under water until it looked like it would sink. One of my buddies asked me, "Do you think it will float?"

This was the moment we had waited for! At a launching, the ship throws up a huge wave as she slides into the water. This wave now started rolling our way, getting larger and larger as it rolled towards us. At the last second, we realized our four foot painter (rope) attached to the pier was too short. The wave rolled over our bow. Again, we went swimming. The boat did not sink but we all had to bail for a half hour to make it seaworthy again. The motor got thoroughly soaked and would not start. We had to paddle one mile against the current back to the boat-yard we had borrowed the boat from. We all agreed it was the best launching we had ever been to.

The field we played softball at was bordered on two sides by an eight foot chain link fence. Once in a while, somebody would hit a ball over the fence into the shipyard. I would always volunteer to go after the ball.

Once in the yard, I could never resist the temptation to roam around this magic place. One thing always puzzled me. If this was such a great place to be, why did all the workers look so mean. Every day, we had regular shipyard cus-tomers. They even looked mean when they came into my parents' store on the way to and from work. When the yard had a layoff or a strike, these customers would say that they would find another job and never work in the yard again. Always, within a matter of months after the layoff or strike was over, they would be back in our store again buying their papers and cigarettes. I used to wonder why they kept coming back since they all acted like they hated the place.

Within two years, I had a job at a parking lot where the workers parked their cars. This made me feel even closer to the yard. I used to listen to the men talk about the yard and dream about the day when I would work there. Years later, I would realize the magic that attracted me as a boy had cast a spell on most of them even though they hated the place.

Near the yard, there was a drawbridge. From the roadway to the water was about sixty feet. In order to prove himself to the older boys in my neighborhood, a younger boy was expected to jump off this bridge. In the summertime quite often a group of boys would walk up to the bridge. The bridge tender tried to discourage the boys from jumping off, but the boys would all line up on the railing and after much kidding and fooling around, they would all jump off, one after the other.

One day when I was about thirteen, I walked up the bridge with them. After a few minutes, they all jumped off. The bridge tender came running out of his house and started yelling at me. I had taken a look down but didn't want to jump. This gave me a good excuse not to jump and I walked back to the beach. The older boys soon showed up and called me chicken. I told them I was going to jump till the bridge tender showed up. They said if you are not chicken, prove it.

So, we all marched back up to the bridge and lined up on the railing. I started getting cold feet again. The other boys started jumping off one by one. Finally, I was the only one left. Just then, the bridge tender came out of his house and started walking towards me yelling. He got closer and closer and I could see he was really mad this time. He was just about to grab me when I jumped. I will never forget what the bridge tender yelled just as I jumped: "Come back here you little bastard". From then on, I was one of the boys. I never told the older boys that if the bridge tender hadn't yelled at me, I probably would never have jumped.

When I was a boy, most of my friends grew up in one parent families. Our neighborhood was a transient area and many marriages broke up from alcohol, WWII, and men moving from shipyard to shipyard.

Some of these young guys ended up in jail. Years later I ran into others working in the shipyard. Some of those guys won parole because the shipyard guaranteed them jobs. I remember two in particular very well. We had been good friends when we were boys, but growing up, we parted ways for various reasons.

One brutally hot night when we were about 14 we decided we would all sneak out of our houses after midnight. We all met at the beach and had a skinny dipping moonlight swim. After hanging out for a while, we decided to walk up to the square to an all night restaurant. By then, it was 3:00 AM. We were having a great time and though we were big wheels staying out all night.

There were no cars around when we started walking. After walking about a mile, we saw headlights approaching. It was a police car. We had not done anything wrong, so we were not scared. The police thought differently. They told us to get in their car and they took us to the police station. One by one, they took all four of us into a small room and questioned us at length. After that, they kept us separate and would not let any one of us talk to any other.

We compared notes later and found that the cops had said the same thing to each of us. They said that your buddy squealed on you and we know about the vandalized cars, breaking and entering, etc. We had not done anything but they were determined to pin something on us that had happened recently. After about one hour, they gave up and realized we were just four young boys who found it too hot to sleep and were out on a great adventure.

They drove us home. Two boys lived across the bridge in the next town so the police dropped them off at the bridge.

Johnny lived near the shipyard with his father. The police said they were going to knock on his door. Johnny was scared of his father. He said, "Please don't. My father will kill me and then have a shit fit." This seemed to amuse the police and one officer said, "What's a shit fit?" Johnny said, "First my father will have a fit and then a shit." The police thought this was hilarious coming from a 14 year old boy. They let Johnny climb in the coal chute window that went into his cellar.

I couldn't think of anything amusing to say when they took me home. The officer and I knocked on the door at about 5 AM. It was daybreak and my poor mother came to the door and said, "Oh David, what have you done?" I was grounded for two weeks, a fate worse than death in the middle of summer.

Many years after that I ran into Johnny in the yard and found out he had been in jail.

I had another buddy back then named Jimmy. He was a big blonde good looking kid, a little on the wild side, but fun to hang out with. I lost track of him growing up. Years later, I was working at a maximum security prison doing new construction. The prisoners would pass by us every day, but we had a prison guard with us at all times making sure there was no contact between us and them.

One day, I heard a loud, very deep voice, yell out, "Hey, Dave"! I turned around and there was this huge blonde guy. He obviously had been lifting weights for a long time. I said, "Jimmy?". He nodded and I said, "What are you doing here?". He said, in that loud deep voice, "Eight to twelve years, armed robbery." The guard told us both to shut up and I waved bye.

Jimmy came to work in the yard a few years later and we had a laugh over that earlier chance encounter after not seeing each other for years.

Shortly after graduation from high school, I was accepted into the apprenticeship program at the shipyard. This was the culmination of a long dream. The apprenticeship program lasted four years. After a thirty day trial program, myself and eleven other boys were dropped from the program. This was quite a blow to me. I wasn't interested in all the book learning in the program and they decided I wasn't interested enough to invest four years training in me. Shortly after that, my family and I moved away from the yard. I went on to other jobs. Every day I passed the yard on my way to and from work. It still fascinated me although I decided it was not for me.

◆   ◆   ◆

Several years later I went back to work at the yard. I planned only on working one winter and going back into construction in the spring.

I took a two dollar an hour cut in pay working there. However, little did I know I would stay there for many years. At the time, they were building submarines. In the following years, they would build many different kinds of ships: destroyers, cruisers, ammo ships, cargo ships, sub tenders, supply ships, container ships, liquefied natural gas ships, and barges.

Pudgy the Wonder Dog

We had a beautiful all white springer spaniel back then. Dead center in that big white back, six inches from that big fan of a tail like somebody painted it, was a six inch black spot. The rest of the body was all white with the exception of the big, black, noble head. From his nose, running up over his head between his eyes, was a white stripe about one inch wide. This was an elegant looking dog, especially with that lacy white tail. The springer breed usually has the tail cut off as a puppy. Almost a sin, since they have a tail like an irish setter or an english setter. Way back in 1945 a hunter offered my parents $50 for the six month old puppy and he didn't even have papers. You could buy a good used car for $100 then.

This was some dog!! When he was a puppy he was heavy, hence the name, "Pudgy". By the time he was two, he had slimmed down, grown up and weighed about 40 pounds.

About this time, he met an enemy that would dog him for the next 12 years. The enemy's name was donuts: chocolate, jelly, lemon, honey dip, strawberry, raspberry, coconut; you name it. He never looked, sniffed, or checked them out. He was not prejudiced. He didn't care what color or kind. They all went down the hatch. Once in a while in one bite, but usually two. If you tried to hold on to the donut, you might lose a few fingers. This was a gentle, affectionate dog except when it came to two things: donuts and other male dogs in his territory.

When he was about two we moved from the country into the city. Our house was only about 600 feet from the shipyard and it had a variety store attached to the front. Within six months of us moving there, this beautiful, graceful, sleek dog started having a weight problem. His name began to fit quite well. He also started disappearing every morning. My father thought he had a girlfriend. We all did. But it wasn't a lady friend, it was those devil donuts.

There were three different bread trucks delivering bread, pastries, and *donuts* to our store every day. He used to climb right up on the trucks and check them out. Each customer or salesman who entered the store was checked out by Pudgy but bread salesmen were given an especially joyous welcome. His tail would practically wag off his backside. That tail wagged for everybody, though, and all our regular customers patted the dog and talked to him.

My father talked to one of the bread salesmen one day and the mystery of the disappearing dog was solved. About one half mile from our store was two other grocery stores. Pudgy would run up to these two stores at 8:00 every morning and catch the bread truck drivers coming out of the stores with day old bread, pastries, and *donuts*. If the driver was in the store, Pudgy would climb up into the truck and wait. The drivers liked it because they liked Pudgy and he would guard the trucks. I knew better. He was guarding the donuts! His pay for guard duty was one half to one dozen day old donuts. He would get a free ride back to our store on the trucks and have donuts on the way.

This dog could even tell time. When the truck made its delivery to our store, he would waddle off the truck and go have a nap and rest up for lunch. Lunch at the shipyard was 11 to 11:30 AM. The lunch whistle would blow at 11:00 AM and Pudgy would waddle down to the shipyard. Many shipyard workers would eat lunch outside the yard sitting on a low fence surrounding the parking lots.

I was curious why he started disappearing at 11:00 each morning, so one day I followed at a discreet distance. What I found was rather shocking. Here my wonderful, well fed dog had become a common panhandler. He was sitting up on his haunches begging food from the shipyard workers. This, only two and one half hours after downing jelly donuts. I honestly believe if you put a ham bone and one half dozen donuts in front of him, he would opt for the donuts. We never taught him to sit up and beg, but apparently he had learned how. He would sit there on his backside with two front paws hanging out, drooling away and looking serious and hungry. The guys used to laugh at the way he begged and he soon had a bunch of them trained to feed him every morning at lunch. When the 11:30 whistle blew, Pudgy would waddle home and wait for the school kids to arrive. But first he would have to have a nap from all his labors.

Our store had two big plate glass windows in front. Between these two windows was a six foot by four foot recessed entryway. Pudgy would usually lay out in front of the store in the shade under the store awning that covered the sidewalk.

The kids got out of school at 2:30 and some would come in the store to buy candy, ice cream, soda, and pastry. When they came to the store, Pudgy would greet them out front with the tail wagging. After they bought their goodies, he would wait outside, sitting up and begging. They all thought this was funny and he would usually get half of their goodies.

If small kids came in the store, he would get up and greet them, too. Then, he would walk over to the entryway and get in position to waylay the small kids coming out the door with their goodies. The scene that would greet these kids coming out the door into this narrow entryway would be this: Pudgy would be sitting up on his haunches blocking access to the sidewalk. The poor little kids would practically have to climb over Pudgy to get to the sidewalk.

One five year old came in one day with a dime and bought a two scoop chocolate ice cream cone. When he went out, he did not carry his cone high enough and Pudgy thought it was for him. He came back into the store bawling and said Pudgy had eaten his ice cream. My father gave him another two scooper and told him to carry it over his head until he got by Pudgy, the Wonder Dog.

After his afternoon nap, Pudgy would wait for the second shift supper whistle to blow at 7:30. Weather permitting, he would waddle down there to panhandle off the second shift guys. For some reason when we put dog food in his dish, he seldom ate it.

I went to junior high school one mile from my house and one and one half miles to high school. We walked to and from junior high and it was not uncommon to see Pudgy a long way from my house out taking a stroll. Sometimes, a mile or more away. Probably looking for a bread truck or donuts. By then, his weight ballooned up to about 80 pounds. So we started keeping him in the yard in the morning until after the bread trucks left.

Soon, my father started getting reports in the store from our customers about Pudgy. His colors were one of a kind and there was no mistaking him for another dog. Customers would report seeing him a mile, a mile and a half, or two miles away.

It was about this time that he started riding city busses. I think between telling time, riding bread trucks, cars, and busses and eating people food, he started thinking he was human. He was a very affectionate dog and loved humans, but did not like other dogs. When they tried to be buddies, he would turn on them. He was human and they were just dogs.

There was a city bus stop in front of our store. Lo and behold one day, the shipyard bus stopped and out waddled Pudgy. No passengers, just my dog. The bus driver closed the door and drove off. This started happening fairly regularly. Like the dog had a job and was coming home from work.

The City of Quincy was the hub of the south shore of Boston. All city busses fanned out from a terminal in Quincy Square. Each bus had a different route and destination. The destinations were printed in large letters on the front of the bus. Some of the destinations were North Quincy, East Weymouth, North Weymouth, Hingham, Abington, Brockton, Nantasket, Shipyard, etc. Sometimes six or more busses would be idling at the terminal (waiting room) and waiting sometimes as long as 20 minutes for their passengers to get on before they left at their designated times.

Now, I knew we had a smart dog. After all, he was "Pudgy, the Wonder Dog" and he could tell time! We all wondered how he knew to get on the shipyard bus as opposed to the other dozen or so busses that all left from this terminal. Then it dawned on me. We all knew he had learned how to tell time and now he had learned how to read. This was amazing to me because I had a buddy that could still not tell time in the eighth grade but I had a dog that could tell time and read. Pudgy, the Wonder Dog. Did I have a very smart dog or a very stupid buddy?

After a few months, the mystery of the literate dog was solved. The next to last stop on the shipyard bus was our store. Some of the drivers would park their busses and walk over to our store for a soda before their next bus run. They were usually the same drivers on the same routes. My father questioned one of the drivers that often drove my dog home. This driver told my father that one day he saw Pudgy wandering around the idling busses and called to him. Pudgy came over and climbed on the bus and lay down by the driver. Shortly thereafter, the bus left the terminal and he got a ride home. This happened many times. All the shipyard bus drivers would drive him home. As far as I knew, he never took a shipyard bus up to Quincy Square. It was always a bus home. I think he probably walked up to the square trying to find the elusive bread trucks. Who knows, maybe he checked out the grocery stores in Quincy Square. He had friends everywhere.

There were a few other dogs in our neighborhood and Pudgy barely tolerated them. After all, they were just dogs and could not tell time or read. He patrolled our neighborhood and other dogs usually stayed in their yards when he was on patrol. He loved to fight and size made no difference to him. Big or small, fat or thin, he would fight them all.

One day, one of our neighbors brought home a big cross breed. He proudly announced it was a cross between a chow and an alaskan husky. This dog quickly started terrorizing the neighborhood. His owner was quite proud of him and loudly proclaimed he had the meanest dog in the neighborhood. Pudgy tolerated him and a couple of times I saw both dogs' hackles go up and thought there was going to be a fight. After about a month, the big dog got braver and braver and ventured further and further into Pudgy's territory. He was much taller than Pudgy and outweighed him by about 25 pounds.

Finally, Pudgy had enough of this new mutt. I was amazed when the big dog snapped at Pudgy. In a flash, Pudgy was on his back, bowled him over, and chewed most of the other dog's ear off. The dog's owner took him to the vet and had him stitched up. Shortly after, the dog disappeared. The owner said the dog didn't like the city and was now living on a farm. Something about him being happier on a farm.

There was one dog in our neighborhood that Pudgy could never beat, though. About three blocks away lived a huge dog named "Major" who was probably more great dane than anything else. He outweighed Pudgy by 30 to 40 pounds and stood head and shoulders over my dog. Major would come into our neighborhood about once a month and pass by my house. He never even came on our side of the street. He was a gentle dog and never made any hostile moves towards Pudgy. Pudgy would spot Major, run across the street, and jump him. The results were always the same. Pudgy would end up on his back, snarling, and Major would stand over him, growling. After a short time, Major would let Pudgy up. Pudgy would trot on home and when he got across the street, he would turn around and bark at Major. Major would just look at Pudgy as if to say, "smarten up", and would trot away.

After living near the shipyard for ten years, my family moved back to the country again. By this time, Pudgy the Wonder Dog was 12 years old. He had slowed down some but was still in good shape. My older brothers were now busy with their lives and Pudgy became my dog. After work on many days I would take him out into the fields and woods chasing rabbits, quail, and pheasants. This was truly his element and he would come home and collapse after our jaunts.

After about two years in the country, Pudgy became ill and hardly moved for two days. Even that beautiful tail stopped wagging. After about two days, he seemed to get a little better and got up. I said, "Come on Pudgy, let's go chase rabbits". He slowly followed me into the woods and we had about a one half hour walk. We saw a couple of rabbits, but the old dog did not have the energy to chase them. We walked on home and the tail started wagging again. When we got home, he lay down on our lawn, wagged his tail a little, licked my hand, gave two big sighs, and that was it. Pudgy the Wonder Dog died and went straight to heaven. A piece of me died that day, too.

In retrospect, from the time I was five years old until I was 19, I had the smartest, bravest, toughest, best looking, and most affectionate dog any boy ever had.

History of the Yard

Any one who is interested in communications and especially telephones is probably familiar with the phrase, "Watson, come here." Thomas Augustus Watson was Alexander Graham Bell's assistant. The phrase, "Watson, come here" is reputed to be the first words spoken over Bell's new invention, the telephone.

Mr. Watson left Bell and eventually settled in East Braintree, Massachusetts, only a short distance from the present location of Fore River shipyard. He dabbled in a few pursuits including farming for a few years before he founded the Fore River Engine Company, builder of marine engines. This little one employee business would eventually become the second biggest shipyard in the United States.

One of the first vessels built at the yard was the lightship *Diamond Shoals*. Lightships were all steel, sometimes double ended (pointed at both ends) and sat high in the water. At one time there were dozens of these rugged little ships anchored off various ports on the east and west coast and also in Europe.

They were floating lighthouses that also had loud foghorns and were usually anchored over dangerous shallow shoals. It was a lonely, dangerous job being stationed at these solitary sentinels. They would stay on station 365 days a year, coming into port only in the worst storms and hurricanes. Because of their locations at these dangerous places, they were sometimes rammed by much larger vessels in the fog or during stormy weather. Some were cut in two and sunk from these collisions.

The same year the lightship was built, the firm broke ground for a bigger shipyard about two miles downriver. This new location had plenty of room to expand and was closer to the ocean. The greater Boston area averages about a 9 1/2 to 12 foot tidal range. In other words, the level of the ocean in Massachusetts Bay and the Fore River goes up and down about ten foot twice a day. This, coupled with the fact that the river was much wider and deeper in this area, would allow the company to build much bigger, deeper draft vessels. ("Draft" is how much of a ship is underwater).

In 1898, the battleship *Maine* was blown up in Havana, Cuba under mysterious circumstances and helped start the Spanish-American war. Soon after, congress authorized the construction of 16 battleships and various other naval ships. Fore River also won contracts for two ships, the *MacDonough* and the *Lawrence*.

The year 1902 was an eventful year for the new company. About this time the name of the company was changed to the Fore River Ship and Engine Company. Two huge ships were launched that year. One was the *Thomas W. Lawson*, named after Thomas W. Lawson, known as the "Boy Wonder of Wall Street". She was the only seven masted schooner ever built and was an awesome sailing vessel in her day. Built as a collier (coal carrying ship), she weighed in at an amazing 5,218 gross tons. Her seven masts were named after the days of the week (Sunday, Monday, Tuesday, etc.). The old Lawson water tower is a prominent landmark in Scituate, Massachusetts. It looks like a medieval tower and is across the street from Lawson's palatial estate called Dreamwold.

The other ship launched that year was the cruiser *Des Moines*. Cruisers were second only to battleships in size and were named after cities while battleships took their names from states. Right outside the main gate of the shipyard is a road named Des Moines Road which, I suspect, was named after this ship.

Before the *Des Moines* could put out to sea on her sea trials, there was one small problem. The Fore River is a boundary between the city of Quincy and the town of Weymouth. Route 3A, a major road from the South Shore to Boston, crossed this river over a narrow wooden bridge. This bridge stood between the *Des Moines* and the ocean and was too small to allow the *Des Moines* through. Everybody, including the cities, the county, and Mr. Watson knew this. Mr. Watson believed the county would build a more modern, larger bridge. They not only decided to build a new bridge but Mr. Watson's yard won the contract to build it.

Shortly before the *Des Moines* went out on trials, Mr. Watson's new swing bridge was floated down the river on barges from the shipyard. This was done at high tide. The bridge was gently lowered onto her new foundations by the falling tides. A short time later, the *Des Moines* passed through. How simple things seemed to be in 1902. Nowadays, the *Des Moines* would sit at the yard for ten years while the politicians argued over the location for a new bridge and who would build it.

In the period 1899–1908, many battleships in the 15,000 ton class were launched, including the *North Dakota, Rhode Island, Vermont*, and *New Jersey*.

During these early years the Quincy yard was building submarines for a small company in Connecticut called the Electric Boat Company. In all, it built 84 subs in Quincy for EBC before EBC even had its own shipyard. In 1904, five subs were built for the Japanese navy to be used in the Russo-Japanese war. After being built, they were disassembled and shipped out west and loaded on freighters for Japan.

Many years later, General Dynamics Corporation would buy Electric Boat in Connecticut. In 1964, General Dynamics bought Mr. Watson's old shipyard in Quincy. And so, after roughly 50 years, Quincy would build submarines again.

In the years before WWI, the new yard constructed many ships of various designs. These included civilian and naval ships (including submarines, battleships, cruisers, and destroyers). One of the battleships built at this time was the *Rivadavia*. She was built for the Argentine navy.

Bethlehem Steel was the chief supplier of steel to the Quincy yard and in 1913 bought the yard and renamed it Bethlehem Fore River. Before the war, the Quincy yard also built subs for England, Canada and Spain. In 1918, a much publicized $10,000 wager was bet between the Bethlehem Quincy yard and the Bethlehem San Francisco yard as to who could build the most destroyers in a given time. It was Quincy, 18 destroyers; San Francisco, six. A lopsided victory for Quincy and San Francisco yard manager Joe Tynan paid off the bet. For good measure, Quincy also built 10 subs and six merchant ships during the same time. Was this a shipyard, or what? Maybe the most amazing shipyard record ever set was set at Quincy and her smaller yard five miles away at Squantum. Squantum is also in the city of Quincy. This record was an astounding 71 destroyers between the two yards in 25 months. More than all other U.S. shipyards combined. One destroyer built at this time was the *U.S.S. Reid.* She was built in the amazing time of 42 days, from laying the keel to delivery. This in addition to the dozens of other vessels, merchant and naval, turned out at the same time at this historic yard. We think we have automation today.

Between WWI and WWII, Quincy continued to grow and prosper, turning out many warships and civilian merchant ships. The Navy's second carrier was built and launched in Quincy in 1925. She was the *U.S.S. Lexington.* Her sister carrier, *Saratoga*, was also launched at another U.S. yard that year. During World War II, we had approximately 125 carriers. Hard to believe. Today we have about 11.

In 1906, Fore River started an apprentice program. They were considered great jobs in their day. Competition to win an apprenticeship was keen. Approximately 15 trades were taught. The young worker toiled for 8,000 hours before he completed his schooling. This program was continued right up until Bethlehem closed the yard about 1960.

The forge at Fore River was the biggest of its type in the United States. It turned out most parts for the ships, including anchors and turrets (guns). At one time, Quincy built everything for its ships: engines, boilers, shafts, anchors, chains, stanchions, even the huge 3, 5, 8, and 15 inch turrets on the destroyers, cruisers, and battleships. Everything, right down to the beautiful all wood liberty boats and whaleboats and the captain's gigs, with all their brightly varnished mahogany trim were carried on board the ships. The forge was in such demand it ran on a six day a week, 24 hours a day schedule.

The tanker, *S.S. Virginia Sinclair* was launched in 1930. Nineteen different ships were built between 1930 and 1933.

The navy's second carrier, the *U.S.S. Lexington,* was built at Quincy. (She was sunk by the Japanese at the battle of the Coral Sea in 1942.)

At that time, Fore River was building two new carriers for the navy, the *Cabot* and the *Bunker Hill.* The workers at the yard were deeply saddened when the *Lexington* was sunk and petitioned the secretary of the navy to change the name of the *Cabot* to the *Lexington* and he went along with it. The new *Lexington* was launched in 1943.

Up until WWII, all carriers had revolutionary war battle names. After running out of Revolutionary War battle names, the navy seemed to have no rhyme or reason as to how they named new carriers. Battleships were still named after states and cruisers after cities. Some carriers were named after prominent people, like the *Cabot* or *Hancock*; others were named after insects, like the *Wasp* or *Hornet.* The *Wasp* was built in Quincy. The *Hornet* became famous because of the Dolittle raid on Tokyo.

After WWII, many ships ordered by the U.S. Navy were canceled. The destroyer, *Joseph P. Kennedy* was delivered in 1945 and at present is a museum ship on display in Fall River, Massachusetts.

From the late 1940s to the mid 1950s, Quincy built at least 24 tankers. During this time, she also built two frigates for the navy, five freighters for the U.S. Maritime Administration, and two graceful passenger liners for American Export Lines, the *Constitution* and the *Independence.* They were delivered in 1951. Almost fifty years later one still carried passengers around the Hawaiian Islands. *Does Quincy build great ships, or what?*

In the late 1950s, Quincy built another three frigates and five destroyers for the U.S. Navy. From the mid 50s to about 1960, Quincy built an additional 17 tankers and, up until that time, the worlds heaviest ship, the 106,500 ton tanker, *Manhattan.* She was later converted to the world's largest icebreaker and made one historic voyage through the Northwest Passage, carrying one barrel of oil, to prove oil could be transported from the new North Slope oil fields to a warm water port.

In 1961, the world's first nuclear powered surface combat ship, the cruiser *Long Beach*, was delivered to the navy by Quincy. It was followed in 1962 by the navy's second nuclear powered surface ship, the destroyer *Bainbridge*. A few freighters were built for the United States Lines in 1963, but with no new contracts, Bethlehem Steel closed the yard.

In 1963, General Dynamics reopened the yard. Under their ownership, many fine ships were delivered. One of the first contracts was to convert four old navy oilers (oil tankers) to *Apollo* tracking ships. These ships were cut in two and a new midsection was added. Many huge radar dishes were installed on the decks of each ship. The ships were all painted white and looked very impressive with those huge radomes.

About this time, two subs were finished in Quincy and two additional subs were built. In the years before the LNGs, Quincy built ammo ships, sub tenders, LSDs (landing ship docks), and AORs (navy oil tankers). All of these ships were built for the U.S. Navy with the exception of the LNGs and the Lykes sea bees (barge carrying ships). After the LNGs, some barges and a collier (coal carrier) were built. Also, six MPS ships were built for the federal government.

With no new contracts after these ships were finished, General Dynamics closed the yard in 1986.

City Within the City

During and right after WWII, there were 32,000 people working at the two shipyards run by Bethlehem Steel. Around the shipyard sprang up a city within the city of Quincy.

This city was comprised of many different stores, restaurants, bars, diners, and multiple housing units. It was a little city serving the shipyard people and their families within the greater city. In our immediate neighborhood were four drug stores, three hardware stores, four grocery stores including an A&P, six variety stores, four clothing stores, two jewelry stores, three car dealers, one used car lot, four barber shops, six gas stations, one auto parts store, two outboard motor shops, one joke shop, three churches, one soda bottling plant, three Chinese laundries, two schools, grades one through six, a library, a movie theater, a pool room, bowling alleys, 11 bars, 12 restaurants, and a curious New England phenomenon called "diners" with probably more right in our area called Quincy Point than anywhere else in New England.

Diners were very interesting restaurants. The original ones were wooden wagons on wheels. Later, they were made in factories of stainless steel and brought to the restaurant site in one piece or sometimes in two pieces like a double wide trailer. They were all natural stainless steel and never needed any painting on the outside, just an occasional wash. Sometimes they had a baked on paint job. Some of the color schemes were quite bright and sometimes they were half natural stainless and half painted. They ranged in length from about 30 feet to over 100 feet. They came from the factory completely assembled with booths and benches, a long counter with stools, beautiful marble counter and tabletops long before Formica counters, and all the restaurant equipment installed and ready to go. Fryolators, ovens, grill, pie cases, exhaust fans, etc. Almost everything was made from stainless steel and easy to clean. If you sat at the counter you would be waited on usually within five minutes.

Within about one mile of the shipyard were five diners. The five were named: Eddie's, Granite City, Sunset, Mayflower, and Presidents. Many shipyard workers ate at these diners, usually before or after their shifts. In the days before fast food restaurants, these were fast and cheap.

18

Some of the bars were real dumps and some of the barmaids also did a little side business. One notable bar was run by three sisters and went by the name "The Three Sisters." Its more commonly known name by the shipyard guys was "The Six Tits".

During and right after the war, there were not only thousands of workers, but hundreds of sailors getting on the ships to go overseas. Most of them were just young kids, 18–20 years old, and many were taken advantage of by some of the more unsavory low lifes that frequented the bars. A few times when I was a kid going to school, I saw sailors passed out in ditches or sitting up against a tree.

At most of the bars a person could make bets on many sporting events and the numbers published in the newspaper were betted on by thousands of people every day. Most people bet a nickel on a number which won you $30.00, right up to 25 cents, a number which paid $150. The betting numbers were three digits (as in 327) and were either the published treasury numbers or the total bet daily at different race tracks around the country.

Betters might place bets on the date of their birthday, such as 3/17, or their wife's or kids' birthday or a wedding anniversary. Some played multiple numbers every day for 25 cents each. This was in the days when men made $2.00 to $2.50 an hour. Almost every day when you came to work right away somebody would ask "What's the number?". Some days there would be a large groan from someone who would say "I played that number every day for six months and it never came in. I stopped playing it last week." It was a real sucker game that I played for about a month when I was a kid before I wised up. Some poor souls played it year in and year out for a lot of money. Other people just played it for a nickel a day and never won but it was fun and something to talk about. It was one of the Mafia's biggest money makers for many years.

It sometimes would be funny listening to a better giving his selection to his bookie and watching the bookie write it in his little book. The better might say "Give me $10.00 on Beetlebomb in the fifth at Hialeah." Some of these bookies spent most of their shift walking around the shipyard collecting money and booking numbers. A person would wonder how they could get away with booking numbers most of their shift and not working much.

Periodically, management would crack down and the bookies would lie low for a while and then in a matter of weeks, you would see them scurrying around again like little rats always looking over their shoulder with their beady little eyes for bosses who might catch them booking. I sometimes wondered if management tolerated it up to a point. Everybody knew who the bookies were and yet they never seemed to get fired.

When I was in my mid teens, I had a good friend named Ikey. Ikey lived with his uncle and aunt. His uncle was one of the biggest bookies in the yard and carried, in those days, what would be considered a huge sum of money: $200 to $500. He used to leave little piles of bills around the house. When my buddies and I planned a trip around town to go roller skating at a rink or to the beach and amusement park, Ikey would usually finance the trip with a $10 or $20 bill from the piles of bills left around his uncle's house. We all thought we were big shots with a $20 bill.

On the way to school, there was a small store with one long counter inside the door. This was a Chinese laundry and their main business was washing and ironing white shirts (before permanent press shirts). If you went by the store any time between six AM and 12 midnight, there would always be someone ironing shirts behind the counter. Right inside the door was a light switch that controlled the one overhead light hanging from an electrical cord. The light was suspended over the ironing board and plugged into it would be the iron and usually a radio. To turn it on and off one had to walk all the way around this ten foot long counter to the door to turn the light on and off.

The door was open a good part of the year to try and get a little breeze into the shop. We used to think it was a great joke to stoop down in front of the store and reach up and turn off the light, iron, and radio. This would cause whoever was ironing to have to come out from behind the counter and turn the switch back on. We used to consider this great fun and would do it once or twice a week. One day I scooted along and just as my hand hit the switch, a ten foot bamboo pole came smashing down on my knuckles. I looked up and the Chinaman behind the counter was having a great laugh, going "He, he, he, he, he!"

For the rest of that day my knuckles and hand were very sore and I could hardly write in school. The next day we took a different route to school.

We had about a one mile walk to school and we used to pick trash put out by people for the city to pick up. We also picked up soda bottles for return. Big ones were worth a nickel and small ones, two cents. Around the gates of the shipyard you could sometimes pick up a quarter's worth of empty drink bottles left by the yardbirds at lunch or supper time.

We used to try and find brass, copper, or lead pipe or any thing made from these materials. On our way, we walked through a Jewish neighborhood. There were two junk dealers there and we would sell our goodies on the way to school for ice cream and candy money. One morning we found a painted hot water tank like the ones people had in their kitchens. They stood about six feet tall and were about 12" to 14" in diameter. Sometimes they were made of galvanized steel and sometimes copper. People usually kept the copper ones highly shined and once in a while painted them. This tank was painted. Herbie always kept a small magnet in his pocket to check steel. When he put it on this tank he proclaimed in a loud voice, "I think it's copper". We scratched some of the paint off and sure enough, it was copper. It took two of us to carry it to the junkies. It probably weighed 50 pounds. We got rich that day.

Another thing we used to do on holy days was turn on lights and stoves for Jewish people. Orthodox Jews were not allowed to use certain modern appliances on holy days. They cheated a little by hiring gentiles to turn them on for them. On holy days the old Jewish ladies would stand in their doorways and ask us to turn on their stove or lights. This was usually good for a nickel or sometimes only two cents.

My biggest money making venture back when I was 11 was working in a ship-yard parking lot. One day I was walking to school with three of my buddies and they stopped and started opening car doors and stealing things in glove boxes of cars. I was scared and kept on walking when a man approached me. I thought we were all going to jail. He asked me where I lived and what my name was. Boy was I scared! Next thing I knew he offered me a job collecting money and putting paid stickers on cars parked in his lot. He told me to come back that day after school and we would talk some more. He never saw my buddies rifling through the cars. I told my buddies about it on the way to school.

After school I was scared my buddies would try to get the job and I ran the whole mile back to the parking lot. The man told me I would work five mornings from 6:15 to 7:00 and be paid $1 a morning. I couldn't believe it! Many men were working for 75 cents to $1 per hour and here was I just a kid making $1 for 45 minutes work.

After working about two weeks, coming in at 6:15, I realized just about no cars came in until 6:30 so I came in then. Now I was making the equivalent of $2 an hour. Boy, did I think I had made the big time! That lot held about 50 cars and on Mondays I would collect a dollar a car per week and put a sticker on the car for that week. Daily parking was 25 cents. Later, I went to work in a much bigger lot that had 600 spaces and I had the main gate and usually about 300 to 400 cars would pass through that gate. At the time I was only 13. On Mondays I was a walking bank: dollar bills in my front two pockets and fives and tens in back pockets. I used to worry about getting robbed. Later, the owner went up to $1.50 a week and did that complicate things! Fifty cent pieces were very common then and I would start out with about $5 worth of quarters and half dollars. By

7:00 I used to feel like I was 10 pounds heavier with all the coins bulging in my pockets.

Another rite of passage as a young boy was to swim out to the raft. The raft was maintained by the city at our public beach. It measured about 15 feet wide by 20 feet long and was anchored what seemed one half mile off shore when the tide was in. Actually, it was no more than 200 feet from shore. When the tide was out, it sat high and dry in the mud.

When we were wee lads of seven or so, we would walk out to the raft in knee deep mud and sit on the raft. Now, the tide takes six hours to come in and six hours to go out, twice a day. Every day! We have all heard the expression, "Time and tide waits for no man". How true. After sitting on the raft for a short while, the tide would slowly start to come in. If you could not swim, you had to go back to shore soon or you would be stranded on the raft for about 12 hours until the next low tide. The water would be about ten feet deep at the raft when the tide was in. If a boy could not swim by the age of seven or eight, the raft was not a healthy place to be when the tide was in. This was when the 12 to 16 year old boys took over the raft and woe be it to any little boy to be on the raft when they arrived.

As soon as they arrived, us younger boys would be thrown in. If we climbed back on, we would be thrown in again and again and again until they got sick of tossing us in. Sometimes, they would see how high they could throw us. When I was eight, I could swim fairly well and started staying on the raft longer and longer on the incoming tides. I would never stay until the tide was high because it was too far to swim to shore.

Girls of any age up to 16 were always fair game on the raft. We boys would always offer them a hand like little gentlemen and pull them onto the raft. As soon as they were on, we would throw them in. Some would swim out to the raft and just hang on and never get up. Some seemed to like getting thrown off over and over. Others would get thrown off and get mad and wait until their tormentor's back was turned and push him in. After that, they would jump in and swim madly for shore.

One of our favorite ways to torment the poor girls was with jellyfish. Early every summer, a type of non-stinging jellyfish would appear in the river by the thousands. They were about the size of dinner plates and probably weighed about one pound or more each. We would scoop them out of the water and throw them at the girls on *our* raft. They sometimes broke on contact and if a piece went down the top front of a girl's bathing suit. That was good for extra points.

We used to like to get 20 to 25 people on the raft and then try to sink the raft on one side. As one side sunk lower and lower underwater, the other side would raise higher and higher. Everyone would start sliding into the water. The trick would then be to get to the high side and hang on and then you were "King of the Hill (Raft)".

This raft was anchored in a tidal river called Town River. In this area, the river was about one half mile wide. It meandered about another mile upstream almost to Quincy Square. About one half mile in the other direction, it joined the Fore River and helped form Quincy Bay. About five miles down the bay was the open ocean.

At the juncture of these two rivers was a huge Proctor and Gamble plant. They made Spic and Span and Ivory Soap amongst other products. Some of the by product of the soap factory floated down the river on some days. Big globs of soapy looking stuff. We used to say it couldn't be polluted with all that soap floating around.

There were other industries on the river including two more small shipyards, a big coal wharf, an electrical generation plant, and two oil tank farms. Our river was so polluted, no clam digging was allowed most of the time.

In the same area were many piers and wharves. We had some great games of tag there and we swam off the wharves and piers. When the tide was out, it was about 20 to 25 feet down to the water and if somebody was about to tag you, you would jump in and then have to climb all the way back up the ladder with the other person close behind still trying to tag you.

One day, a huge piling from one of these piers came floating down the river on the outgoing tide. It was 25 to 35 feet long. It was bobbing along at a pretty good clip with the current. We all jumped in and decided to ride it on the outgoing tide. Other boys and some girls jumped in and we soon had 10 to 12 boys and girls all riding down the river. After we rode about one half mile, we went by the P&G plant and on into the bay on our new "yacht". Some kids jumped off and swam into the P&G piers. Us fools stayed on and went into the bay. Part way down the bay, we decided to try to paddle our yacht into shore, but the current was too strong and we had to swim maybe one half mile to shore and then walk barefoot back about two miles on hot city streets to our home beach.

There is an expression, "God protects fools and drunks". To this, I would add, "...and boys". About the age of 12 to 13, to be one of the guys, you were expected to swim the river. This was a commercial river with oil tankers, tugs, barges, lobster boats, and other sundry craft. It was about one half mile across and was not a bad swim. The hard part was coming back as you would be tired.

Next to the P&G plant was a Mobil (Exxon) oil tank farm. Downriver was an independent oil company tank farm. The day I first swam the river a big 600 foot tanker with three tugs was turning the corner at the P&G plant, heading our way. One of the older boys said it was a Mobil tanker. This meant it would tie up at the Mobile tank farm and would not come by our beach. The older boys assured us it would be a safe time to swim the river and off we swam; about six of us.

It took about 15 to 20 minutes to get out to the channel (dredged, deep part) of the river and that's when we realized that this 600 foot long tanker was coming our way and not tying up at the Mobil oil dock. It was moving very slowly in the narrow channel, but still faster than I could swim. When we swam a long distance like that, we would swim maybe 500 feet and then stop and rest and tread water for a few minutes.

I was right in the middle of the channel, resting, when we realized this ship was not stopping at the Mobil dock. A 600 foot tanker from any angle is a huge object. From my vantage point one foot above sea level, it was at least 600 foot high and about one and one half miles long. By this time, they were about 1,000 to 1,500 feet away from us and spotted us in their path. One of the tugs let go a toot on its whistle and then another one did. Boy, did we swim! It still wasn't fast enough for them and the oil tanker let out a blast on her horn. It was so loud, it felt like the water was vibrating. New Olympic records were set that day by six very scared young boys swimming like outboard motors.

We finally made it into shallow water on the other side and collapsed on the beach. At railroad crossings, the signs used to say "Stop, Look, and Listen". Before we swam back that day, we looked and looked up and down that river and listened for any traffic.

When we got back to our home beach, we found out we had made some people on the beach very worried. They knew we were swimming across and had seen and heard the oil tanker. They could just barely see our heads from the beach and the next thing they knew, the tanker was passing by where we had just been. It was long, anxious minutes before the 600 foot long tanker passed by and they could then see us on the beach. We were so far away, they couldn't tell if we had all made it.

Long before the shipyard started building ships, Quincy was known far and wide for another reason: granite. Quincy granite was quarried in the south and west parts of the city in open pit quarries. Some of them were hundreds of feet deep. Eventually, they filled in with water, usually spring water and rain water. It is probably the cleanest, freshest water a person could swim in.

One of the oldest quarries in the city was still being worked when I was about 12 years old. My junior high school science class went on a field trip to this quarry. It was located on a hill hundreds of feet high. As a result of its location on this hill, they had been able to cut granite hundreds of feet down without running into water.

The quarry workers were lowered down to the bottom every morning in a steel bucket hooked up to a crane. Our guide at the quarry said the men were working at the 400 foot level and pointed them out to us. They looked like ants. Thirty foot ladders going from one ledge to another looked like toothpicks. I was in awe of the whole operation and a bit scared looking over the edge.

Our guide told us a very interesting story about cutting granite. In the old days, when most things were done by hand, if they wanted to split a piece of granite, say 10 X 10 X 10, a series of small holes would be drilled in a straight line across the stone. Into these holes a series of <u>oak</u> wedges would be driven in and then water poured over the wedges until the holes were filled with water. In time, the wood wedges would swell and the granite would split.

About two miles from my house was an abandoned quarry that had filled in with water. This quarry was unique in that a person could walk in without having to jump off a ledge. Of course, when you walked in, when you got about waist deep, the bottom dropped off to who knows what depth, maybe 100 to 200 foot deep. Not a very good place for a novice swimmer! When I was a young boy of eight, I learned how to swim in a quarry. It was sink or swim.

The quarry was aptly named, "Echo Lake". When a person swam out to the middle and yelled, his voice would bounce off the granite walls and echo back and forth. Unlike most quarries, this one was cut into the side of a hill. It was almost round and about 250 to 300 feet in diameter. On one side, the water was ground level. Gradually, the sides of the quarry got higher and higher until on the far side, it was about 70 feet down to the water. There were different spots to jump into the quarry and each ledge had a different name. Some industrious person had measured the distance down to the water and painted names and heights on the granite. Some of the names were "Betsy 26'"; "Shelve 35'"; Running Shelve 20'"; "Path 48'"; and the king of them all, "Razzle Dazzle 70'". The highest I ever jumped was "Path". When I hit the water, my bathing suit ended up around my neck.

Granite from these quarries was used all over New England for building foundations; road curbings (in New England, curbings have to be granite to withstand snow plow blades bouncing off them when the streets are plowed); facades of high rise buildings; statues; monuments; and tombstones.

The very famous Minot's Ledge lighthouse, about one mile out to sea from Cohasset, Massachusetts, is Quincy granite and so is the Bunker Hill monument in Charlestown, Massachusetts. Bunker Hill is where the revolutionary war battle of the same name was fought. This is the battle where the American commander said to the patriots, "Don't fire till you see the whites of their eyes".

Minot's light flashes 1–4–3 and is known as "Lover's Light". From the shore, it is very bright and prominent. Lovers parked along the shore in autos have decided 1–4–3 means "I love you".

Late every winter we would check our favorite swimming holes, fresh and salt water, to see if the ice had melted. If the ice went early, we would try to be the first ones in swimming that year. This was good for bragging rights. One warm Valentine's Day in the late 1940's, we walked up to Echo Lake. Much to our surprise, the ice had melted, but to only about 30 foot from shore.

The temperature was probably about 45 to 50 degrees and we all decided to go in. We didn't know anybody that had ever gone swimming before Valentine's Day. We were sure we were setting a new record and would have big time bragging rights.

We all stripped down and jumped in. Boy, was it cold! Only about 30 feet away, the ice still covered the whole quarry. Within two days, a story hit the newspaper that made us cringe. A body had been found in Echo Lake, about 50 feet from shore at the edge of the ice. Probably 25 feet from where we had been swimming. The murder victim was a Boston used car dealer and had been shot. The body was weighed down with a section of railroad track and had only recently come to the surface. This was back in the days when you hardly ever read about a murder in the newspapers. When a murder happened, it would be in the paper for a week or more. Here again, the expression, "God protects fools and drunks and young boys", seems apt.

Another good way to make money when I was 13 to 16 years old was setting up pins at a bowling alley. It was hard work, but good money.

New England, and especially Massachusetts, has a different way of bowling than anywhere else in the United States. The pins are called "candle pins" and look like candles. They stand about 16 inches tall and are about 3 inches in diameter. Three balls are used per frame. The balls are about one and one half times the size of a softball. They look and feel like three pound cannonballs and are bowled or thrown down the alley very much like any other bowling ball, with one notable exception: *speed!*

Some people throw these three pound balls at about the same speed as the big balls. Others throw them a little faster and some throw much, much faster. Try

50 to 60 MPH! This cannon ball then becomes a deadly missile aimed down the alley at the pins and sometimes the helpless pin boys. In candlepin bowling, if all the pins are knocked down with one ball, it is a strike. If it takes two balls to knock down all the pins, it is a spare. If pins are still left standing after two balls are thrown, then a third ball is thrown. Whatever pins are left standing after three balls are thrown are subtracted from the ten standing originally and that is your score for that frame. This makes for much lower scores. A man with a 100 average would be considered a good bowler. An average of 110, expert. Around 120 would be a pro.

Before automated pin setting machines were invented, young boys would set up the pins. About as hard, hot, and hazardous job as one could have. A pin boy would sit right in the center, about 3 1/2 feet, above two alleys. When the pins were knocked down, you would jump into the pit, retrieve the ten pins, and stand them all up on the spots on the alley. As you were setting them up, the pins would be knocked down in your other alley. Meanwhile, pins would be knocked down in the adjacent two alleys on either side of you. Fast bowlers would throw the balls so hard the pins would fly through the air, sometimes right up to where you were sitting. Almost as often as the pins came flying, the balls would come flying too. Sometimes right at your face. You would constantly be fending off pins and three pound cannon balls with your legs, feet, hands, and elbows. It was dangerous! My older brother had two front teeth knocked out setting up pins. If a fast bowler missed an easy spare on his second ball, then he would throw the third ball down at what seemed 100 MPH almost like he was mad at the poor pinboy.

We were paid the princely sum of seven cents a string. From 7:00 to 8:30 PM, I would set up 30 strings and from 9:00 to 10:30, another 30 strings. Sixty strings in all at seven cents a string was $4.20. On top of that, about $2.00 in tips for a total of about $6.00. Big money! Hard work! and lots of black and blue marks. Today, they probably would not allow pin boys. It would probably be called exploiting children or cruelty to children. We called it Big Money. God protects drunks, fools, and young boys.

It always seemed I got my heaviest school homework load on nights when I set up pins. Needless to say, I skipped my homework because I needed the money for my latest and most manly habit: smoking cigarettes. Now, I was really a big shot. I had my own cigarettes and didn't have to bum them off my buddies. (By 14, I was smoking a pack a day.)

The man who ran the bowling alleys was a short, very emotional Italian man with a bad temper. He had a constant battle recruiting and keeping dependable pin boys. One night, I was scheduled to set up pins for a league and couldn't make it. I made the mistake of personally going to the alleys and telling him I would not set up pins that night. I should have called instead. He started yelling and cursing me out and I yelled back at him. Next thing I knew, he came after me.

The ten bowling alleys were located under the Lincoln movie theater. There were about twenty steps leading up to the street. I went flying up the steps at 100 MPH with the manager in hot pursuit. I hit the door running and threw it open. Just on the other side of the door was a Quincy cop. Not just any cop, but one with a tough, mean reputation. He went flying and landed on his butt. I never looked back and kept running.

I found out a few days later that he had his glasses on and was carrying a cup of coffee in one hand and a newspaper in the other hand. He was coming down to the alleys for a coffee break with his paper. When he fell, his glasses went flying and he stepped on them. For months later, when I saw him walking his beat I would cross to the opposite side of the street. As far as I know, he never knew who I was. Lucky for me!

On the second floor of our house there was a three room apartment and three single rooms that my family rented out to shipyard workers. When the luxury liners *Independence* and *Constitution* were being built, in the late forties and early fifties, we rented the upper floor to some of the ships' officers. I believe they were the first and second mates and the ships' purser amongst others. A few months after they moved in, we had a minor smoky fire in the refrigerator on the second floor. They had to pass through this smoky kitchen to get out the exterior door of the house. They were absolutely terrified by this minor, smoky fire. I thought it was very exciting. The big red fire truck, siren and all.

A few days later, they told my parents why they had been so scared of this fire. Some of them had been on an oil tanker that caught fire and sank at sea. Before the sinking, oil spilled out from the tanker onto the sea and caught fire. With the flaming ship sinking, they had been forced to jump overboard into the flaming sea and swim for a lifeboat. They had to swim underwater to avoid the fire and came to the flaming surface to take a breath and then dive under again to swim to the lifeboat. Some of their crew members didn't make it. The ones who did make it were burned, some much worse than others.

I remember as a young boy being terrified when told this story. I did not know oil would burn on top of water and the idea of the ocean being afire was scary to me, especially having to swim in it.

Back then there were hardly any cars on the road. There were no civilian cars produced from 1941 to 1945. Gas was on ration and a person was only given enough to get back and forth to work. Most people went to work on public transportation.

There were so many men working in the yard during and right after the war that the local bus company put on dozens of extra busses and trolley cars every day. The trolleys ran right down the middle of the streets on railroad tracks. They had huge metal wheels with a flange that ran in a groove on the tracks. The streets the trolleys ran on had overhead wires suspended from one side of the street to the other. Another wire, which was electrified, ran across these wires down the middle of the street. On the back of the trolley, sticking up like a flagpole, was a rod that ran up to this wire. Current was carried from the wire down the pole into the trolley car and to its electric motor.

One of our little tricks to aggravate the trolley operator was to pull this rod down from the overhead wire. We would jump on the trolley and if it did not make a stop near where we wanted to get off, we would pull the rod down. This would break the electrical connection to the overhead wire, the trolley would slow down, and we would jump off and run before it stopped. The poor motorman would get out of the trolley, walk around back, and have to put the rod back on the overhead wire. Other times, we used to hop on the back outside of the trolley when it made a stop and hang on and go for a ride, free. To say he was mad would be an understatement. Nice kids!!

As the trolleys traveled along their routes all over the city, they made a loud screeching noise, especially going around corners when the metal wheels would bind up on the railroad tracks. After dark the wheels threw up lots of sparks. The sparks were tiny compared to the sparks the overhead rods made on the connection to the overhead wire. The trolley would scream and whine, lurching around the city with sparks shooting out overhead and sparks coming off the wheels. Quite a noise and sight, especially after dark.

Nicknames, Aliases and Who Knows

If you were brought up in the forties, fifties, or sixties, you have probably seen the "Kilroy was here" logo. It first started showing up all over Europe and the pacific during WWII. It consisted of a face with a big long nose and two large round eyes. The nose and face were hanging over a wall and sometimes the fingers of both hands would be shown gripping the top of the wall. No other parts of the body would show over the wall. The expression, "Kilroy Was Here" would always accompany the drawing.

This logo was sometimes found by GIs when they first entered a newly liberated city in Europe. In WWII, GIs rushed to be the first to put the Kilroy logo everywhere they landed. It would show up in the most unlikely spots and would sometimes be found in areas that had been occupied by the Germans or Japanese. Hitler became obsessed with the "Super GI" who showed up in the most top secret German installations. He became convinced that Kilroy was a super spy and could infiltrate the most top secret German installations. He became so obsessed with it he ordered his best men to try to capture this super spy.

The logo has been found on the arch of triumph in Paris, the George Washington Bridge in New York, and written in dust on the moon. At the Potsdam Conference in 1945, a toilet was built especially for Churchill, Roosevelt, and

Stalin. Stalin was the first one to use it and when he came out, he asked an aide who Kilroy was.

The American Transit Association sponsored a radio program called, "Speak to America". In 1946, the Association held a nationwide contest to try to determine who the real Kilroy was. As a result of the contest, it was determined that the real Kilroy was none other than James J. Kilroy of Halifax, Massachusetts. He was an inspector of the riveting gangs in the Fore River shipyard during WWII. He would count the amount of rivets done by various crews and then leave scribbled in bright yellow chalk the words, "Kilroy was Here" on the steel. The riveters were paid by the amount of holes filled. By writing, "Kilroy Was Here", Jim Kilroy was proving to his bosses that he was on the job. It also stopped unscrupulous riveters from having the same holes counted twice and being paid double.

Ships were leaving Quincy so fast during the war that in many cases, Kilroy's words and logos were never painted over. So the logo traveled all over the world and was copied by GIs in every port or city they landed in.

The American Transit Association presented to Mr. Kilroy a prize of a 22 ton streetcar which Kilroy placed in his yard and converted into sleeping quarters for his children.

I worked with the same people on and off for years at different shipyards. Most of them were good guys. A few were <u>bad</u> actors. Many that I worked with had nicknames and some had aliases. This was before drug screening and checking for police records, a time when companies did not check a man's background. It was especially true if he had worked in another yard and could do the work. Some guys would not talk at all about their background, family, etc. They would be secretive and even if you worked with them for months, they would never open up. They might say they had worked in Charleston, San Diego, Tampa, Boston, and many other places. If you asked them when, they would clam up. Some of them were jailbirds and some had skipped out on their families, alimony, and child support. Some of these guys you would not want to get friendly with.

There were all kinds of eccentrics operating in the yard. I never knew a place with such a cast of characters. They all had nicknames. I knew some of them for years and never knew their real names. There was "The Wharf Rat", "Maury the Midget", "The Bag", "Lester the Molester", "The Wolf Man", "The Glick", "The Fink", "Satch", "Mumbles", "Jack the Greek", "Harry High Pockets", "Bad Frank", "Good Frank", "The Chicken Man", "Eskimo", "Mad Russian", etc. They all earned their names from some peculiar quirk of theirs. We had one boss known as "Ho, Ho, Ho" after the Jolly Green Giant.

We had a boss that constantly checked his men and became a real pain in the neck. He was given the nickname "Mother" and did not like it. His men called him by his first name, but some other tradesmen called him Mother. I was his working leader for about a year and he was a difficult man to work for. When he had a particularly bad job for me he would say, "Davy Baby, have I got a job for you". My whole crew would laugh. I quickly cured him of this. When he said those words, I would bend over with my rear facing him! The crew would laugh again. So much for "Davy Baby".

We had a carpenter called Jeff. One day we needed some staging moved. Mother called the carpenter shop and they sent Jeff over. Mother was busy when Jeff arrived in our area. He waited patiently and finally yelled, "Mother, what staging do you want moved?" Mother ignored him and Jeff yelled it again, louder. Poor Mother looked at him and said, "Who are you calling Mother?" Jeff looked at him and said, "You, you f———a———." Mother looked at him and said, "You can't talk to me that way". Jeff said, "F—y—". By this time, half the crew was watching and laughing. Mother backed off and we got our staging moved.

Jeff, the carpenter, was also known as "Jeff the Rag Man". Jeff could get you any kind of clothes you wanted, cheap. Shirts, pants, overcoats, coats, and rain gear, all second hand and cheap. One day he sold a man a heavy work coat for seven dollars. The man was laid off a short time later and the Rag Man took the coat out of the laid off worker's locker and sold it to another guy for five dollars. It got to be a joke around the yard and we figured he might eventually get $50 for the coat. The second man took the coat aboard ship and that was the end of the coat, or so we thought. That summer, the Rag Man was under the ship moving stagings around and found the coat in a pile of rubbish. He took it home, had his wife wash it, and sold it again.

There was also a man on the other shift who sold second hand clothing to those workers. He was known as, "George the Rag Man".

One of the riggers in our area was a little guy about five feet, four inches. When he was in a hurry, he used to scurry along like a little rat. We called him, "The Wharf Rat". He was a good guy and a very hard worker but also a practical joker. He used to pull practical jokes on me occasionally. One night I decided to get even. Our two cranes moved a big unit about the size of a house and placed it on four pedestals about six feet off the ground. The Rat got a 25 foot ladder and climbed to the top of the unit to take the cables that were hooked to the cranes off the unit. When he was up there, I ran over and took the ladder and hid it under the unit. I then stood under the unit out of the Rat's vision. He thought it was funny at first, but after 10 to 15 minutes and a cigarette, he started yelling at people walking by and asking for a ladder. I would start to get the ladder and they would see me and keep walking. After an hour, I let him down.

We had a boss called "Lester" and for no apparent reason, he won the nickname "Lester the Molester". We had another boss named "Doucette". People called him "The Bag" behind his back. I could never figure this one out until I heard somebody call him the "Douche Bag" one day.

One little guy was called "Maury". He wasn't big enough to do the heavy physical work demanded of the shipfitting trade. He quickly started sucking up to our foreman and was nicknamed, "Maury the Midget", or "Brownie", for obvious reasons. He eventually got a "chaser" job in our department. He would check when we would receive stock. He was good at this job and helped us get our material.

We had a man working near us in another department. I never knew his name. He was the hairiest man I ever saw. In the summertime, wearing a t-shirt, he looked like a gorilla. He answered to the name "Wolfman".

There was another guy working with us for a while who was a squealer. He would tell the bosses anything they wanted to know. He was called the "Fink". He transferred off the second shift on to days. I was told somebody beat him up on the second shift. Good riddance!

One of my all time favorite names on the second shift was a man called "Harry High Pockets", or "High Pockets" for short. Harry stood about six foot six and had very long legs. It was said he bought four foot pants and two foot shirts.

We had two Franks on our crew for a while. They became known as "Good Frank" and "Bad Frank". Talk about opposites! The work we did was not only heavy but, at times, dangerous. Because of this, we usually had men working in pairs. Bad Frank was a grouch and lazy. Good Frank was good natured and a good worker. I often had a hard time getting someone to work with Bad Frank. One night was usually enough for everyone. They would refuse to work with him the next night and would say they would rather work alone than with that guy.

There was a big wheel in the yard who closely resembled Frank Perdue of Perdue Chicken fame. His name was Joe Smith but he became known as the "Chicken Man". He walked very fast and would practically run around the yard. You never knew where or when or what shift he would show up on.

He was a fanatic on productivity and was always trying to find guys goofing off. He had the authority to fire bosses at will. If he caught workers loafing he often would fire the boss in charge of these men. Most of the bosses were terrified of the Chicken Man. If he was spotted in our area, we would start chanting "Bok, bok, bok, bok" like a chicken or crowing like a rooster.

"Mother" was worried when Chicken Man was around and we quickly found out how terrified he was. He would panic. Sometimes just to give Mother a hard time, I would tell him the Chicken Man was in the area. He would rush around telling everyone to stay on the job and don't take a coffee break or go to the toilet. Within ten minutes, he would be back and ask where the Chicken Man was. I would say the last time I saw him he was heading towards the steel mill.

We had another boss known as "Ho, Ho, Ho" after the Jolly Green Giant. He was six foot eight inches tall and when he was in the area, the guys would all signal one another by going "Ho, Ho, Ho".

The company would make periodic raids on the rest rooms and isolated areas where workers goofed off. They would no sooner find one area and raid it and the loafers would find another area to goof off.

Our trade consisted of a lot of heavy work. A lot of the tools we used were heavy. As in most jobs, there were short cuts and easier ways of doing things. Some men learned quickly and some never learned. The most common tool to our trade was a sledgehammer. They were issued in sizes from 6 pound up to 16 pound One man on our crew always used a 16 pound hammer. If we showed him an easier way to do a particular job without using his hammer, he would agree wholeheartedly. As soon as you left, he would go right back to his 16 pound hammer and start swinging away again. This may not sound bad, but we used to show him easier ways not just for his sake but also for ours. If you are working in an area where somebody is swinging a sledge hammer, it is noisy. Especially if the steel is thin. The thinner it is the more it rings. After a short time, it does a number on your ears.

One day, he was really pounding out a storm with his hammer when everybody, including him, stopped for coffee. We went over and welded his hammer to the deck. After coffee, he found it and didn't say a word. He just went over to his tool box and got a 10 pound hammer. Now with a 10 pound hammer, you have to hit an object almost twice as much as you would with a 16 pound hammer. We now had more noise than before. At lunch time, we welded this hammer down. After lunch he came back with an 8 pound hammer. At afternoon coffee, we welded his tool box shut. The following day, the boss told us to lay off. He also said that "Harry the Hammer" was one of the best workers he had and all the noise he made sounded good up at the front office. He said no matter where you were within a quarter mile of our area you could hear Harry's hammer ringing. The next day, we all wore ear plugs and as long as Harry the Hammer was on our crew, we continued to wear them. The company loved this as we were supposed to wear them all the time anyway.

There was another man who was known as "The Mad Russian" or "The Eskimo". All spring, summer, and fall he only wore a t-shirt. Even if it got down to 40 degrees. In the winter, he wore a flannel shirt over a t-shirt, but never a coat. On cold days, I wore long underwear, top and bottom, a heavy flannel shirt, an insulated, hooded sweatshirt, and a heavy navy or army watch coat over the sweatshirt. This was about what most men wore, especially on the second shift. The temperature would frequently get down to ten degrees and colder: many nights with a 20 to 25 MPH breeze. Probably a wind chill factor of 20 or 30 degrees below zero. The Mad Russian would go walking by just wearing his shirt. I used to get cold just watching him. Many years after I left the yard, I heard The Mad Russian caught a cold and died from pneumonia.

"Mumbles" was another interesting character. He would start telling you a story and you would understand every word, at first. The longer the story went though, the more he would start to mumble and even more maddening, his voice would drop. I used to think I was going deaf. If you asked him to repeat what he said he would become annoyed. If you asked him to repeat it a second time, he would always say "You smell like a goat". Then when you stood there with your mouth open wondering if you did smell like a goat, he would say "Heard that, didn't you?"

The worst part of the cold was trying to keep your hands and feet warm. The best thing that ever came out in foot gear was skimobile boots with their heavy felt inner socks. I have seen men wear baggies, wool socks, cotton socks, newspapers, women's nylon stockings, you name it, and your feet would still be cold. The company would try to stop us from wearing the skimobile boots because they had flimsy nylon sides and did not have steel toes. If your feet are not warm, it's tough working.

Besides the burners working in our area, there were men called straighteners. They used a big torch with a water line mounted on top of the torch. They would heat steel until it was cherry red and then turn on the water while another man would hit the hot spot with a hammer. To me, a thoroughly boring and <u>hot</u> job. A good job in winter with the big warm torch, but horrible in hot weather.

During my 30 day orientation as an apprentice, one of the instructors, who usually got the instructor's job by who he knew, and not what he knew said, at the end of the class: "Are there any questions? Don't be afraid to ask questions, as there is no such thing as a stupid question." I raised my hand and asked him a question about the homework assignment. He replied, "Now that is a stupid f___ing question"

Most mechanics worked on what was called "The Ticket". A ticket was a description of the assignment and an estimate of how many hours it should take to complete. If the job was completed in less than the estimated time, the mechanic got a bonus. Most tickets had two or three mechanics working on them. Any time that a mechanic was not working on the ticket, he would tell the ratesetter to sign him out because idle time would eat up hours, otherwise called, "Killing the ticket". One time a mechanic who was working a ticket got injured. The crane carried him off the ship in a stretcher. As he was being lowered towards the ambulance, a voice from the assembled crowd shouted out, "Take him off the ticket."

There was a mechanic who was about six foot three and weighed less than 140 pounds. Obviously, he was very skinny. Additionally, he had very narrow shoulders. Actually, it looked like his arms came out of his neck. Looking at him straight on, somebody dubbed him "Chalkline". That name stuck forever.

The shipyard, in the late fifties or early sixties, decided that it took supervisors too long to get from ship to ship or ship to shop. Their answer was to buy each a bicycle. The supervisors didn't think much of this, but they were instructed to use them. There was a leading man in the Outside Machinist's department who was slightly feminine, prudish, and quite meticulous in his manner of speaking. He was known as "Mother". Of course, no one ever called him that to his face. After week or so of the supervisors using their bikes (each bike had their name on it), the night shift got hold of Mother's bike and removed the cross bar between the seat and handlebars, converting it into a girl's bike. Mother loved that.

The Groton, Connecticut shipyard sent what was to be their savior to the yard. He was proclaimed as all knowing and would lead us into new and profitable areas. Unfortunately, this management giant was about five foot one. One day somebody got into his car in the shipyard and left a very large, oversize cushion on the front seat and taped blocks to the brake pedal.

There was a man who was the foreman of the machine shop. He was quite portly and was near bald. He had protruding ears like a loving cup. He was known as "Wingnut".

The guy that sold and fixed watches was known as "Tick Tock".

The guy who roamed the yard looking to kiss young boys was known as "Yum Yum".

The night superintendent of the yard had a reputation as a real rat. You didn't ever want to have him catch you doing something you weren't supposed to be doing. Sleeping in the toilet or even reading a newspaper in the toilet was a real no-no. One night, he suspected that somebody was sleeping in one of the stalls and banged on the door and told the sleeper to open the door. The sleeper looked down and recognized the shoes the super was wearing. He opened the door quickly, kept his head down so he wouldn't be recognized, and took a swing at the superintendent, knocking him out cold. The story goes that he was never caught because the super couldn't identify him.

There were some men who had little in the way of class. In the central toilet, I saw a man going into the toilet to sit. He also used this time for a coffee break since in his hands was a donut and a cup of coffee. (Talk about eating at the "Ritz"!)

There was a leading man in the OSM department who was a rather crude and disgusting person. He chewed tobacco and would spit any time or any where, right on the floor, whether or not you happened to be eating lunch.

He called everyone "Swede" no matter who they were. He also wasn't the brightest bulb in the array. How he ever got a leadingman position, I'll never know. The story goes that he told one of the mechanics to lay out a ship foundation and drill a bolt hole every ten degrees on the circular fdn. The mechanic was looking for more information prior to proceeding. One question led to another and the mechanic happened to ask the leadingman if he knew how many degrees there were in a circle. Perplexed, he answered, "Swede, there must be a million of them".

I worked with a guy who was a heavy drinker and a heavier smoker. He would come in every Monday morning after a rough weekend with a cup of coffee and always a raspberry turnover. One Monday morning, after an especially bad weekend, he was standing next to a tool bench with a cup of coffee and his raspberry turnover, with a cigarette going and proceeded to have a smoker's coughing jag. After a few minutes of coughing, he looked at me, hardly able to talk, and said, "Dave, these things are going to kill me some day." Assuming he was talking about the cigarettes, I asked him why he didn't quit smoking. He said, "I'm talking about the turnovers."

Pete the Polack was a master at getting off difficult jobs at work. We were all first class mechanics, making the same money and equally qualified. When Pete would get a difficult job he would go to the job and start it and then stand there looking perplexed. Usually within a short time one of the boys would come by and see Pete standing there. Pete would say, "I'm having trouble with this job".

He pulled this on all of us. Most men are usually willing to give someone a hand. It is also good for your ego if someone says they have a difficult job and can't do it. Especially if you can do it. Pete was sly and realized this. The gullible one who fell for Pete's helpless bit would usually end up doing the whole job while Pete watched. We all helped him many times.

I did one day. I finished his job and then didn't have enough time for mine. The boss was unhappy because I had not finished an easy job. To add insult to injury, he commended Pete for doing an excellent job. We finally realized we were being had by Pete and everybody agreed we would not help him any more. It came as an awful shock to him when nobody would help him anymore and he had to do his own work. He had been getting by with the little ploy for so long he just could not understand why we would no longer help him.

"Jack the Joker" was a practical joker on our crew who was constantly pulling sick jokes on people. One day he came over to us in great pain. He had his hand up to his eye. Protruding between his fingers was the end of a welding wire. Somebody ran to call First Aid. We all thought he had a welding wire in his eye. When the man ran to call First Aid, Jack quickly dropped the wire and started laughing. He was always pulling sick jokes of this type. We quickly got wise to him but new workers in the area were always falling for his schemes.

One of his jokes finally backfired on him. We had a new welding boss in the area. A crane was lowering a heavy piece of steel onto a platform. The riggers and this joker were guiding it into place. When the steel touched down, the joker let out a horrible scream. He took off his glove and the tips of his fingers were covered with blood. The welding boss came running over, took one look, and I thought he was going to pass out. He ran for the office and called First Aid. When he came back, the joker was washing off his hand. What everybody had thought was blood was ketchup. Before he had put on his glove, he had poured a lot of ketchup into the glove. By this time, it was too late and the First Aid man was on the way. When he arrived on the scene and found out what had happened, he was furious. The joker was told if he ever pulled another joke like this he would be fired.

We used to be given a half day off before Christmas and were supposed to *work* a half day. We usually started off working, but after an hour or so, people would start socializing and partying, including drinking. The company decided after a few years to give us the whole day off since not much work was done anyway.

I remember an incident that happened on the second shift when we were still working the half day before Christmas. We started work as usual at 3:30 and a short time later, we opened the riggers' locker to get some equipment. This was a big stand-up locker about seven feet high by six feet wide and about three feet deep. Sitting there, half buried by rope and chain, was a young first shift rigger. The whole locker reeked of alcohol. He had drunk too much at a Christmas party and passed out in the locker.

His brother Eddie worked on the second shift with us and he was summoned. Eddie told his brother to stay in the locker until 7:30 when we all would be going home; about two hours later. The young rigger decided to go home right away. You could not leave the yard without permission from your supervisor and the guards would not let you exit the gate without permission. This rigger decided he was going to sneak out and would go over the fence. He was still not functioning too well and a second shift boss chased him down. The boss brought him to the second shift superintendent and he was given a chit and time off without pay.

Later that night we were at a local bar, still celebrating, when the boss who caught the rigger came in. He went up to the bar and started drinking. I yelled out from our table, "Jones is an a__hole!." He turned around and asked, "Who said that?" Bill, the burner, pointed to me. The boss came storming over and asked why I said that. I replied, "Because you are. Why didn't you escort the rigger to the gate and let him go home, especially it being the day before Christmas?" We had a few more words and he left realizing that the other bar patrons heard what he had done. Because of this and other incidents, he became so hated that after his car was vandalized a few times, the company allowed him to park in the yard.

For about a year, I worked with a rigger named Dick Leadgood who was quite a character. He was originally from the island of Nantucket, Massachusetts. After WWII, he was mustered out of the army in Virginia. Having grown up near the ocean and being a commercial fisherman, he was fascinated by boats. The amphibious army vehicle known as a "duck" intrigued him. While still in Virginia, he decided to buy a surplus duck. I asked him if it was difficult getting it registered. He said, "Hell, no. I didn't bother." It still had its military paint job and he still had his army fatigues. Dressed in fatigues, he drove it on the highway from Virginia to Massachusetts.

Dick and his duck were a very unusual sight on the highway. When he got pulled over by the cops, he would explain that he was on active duty delivering the duck to an army base. As it turned out, in most cases, the cops were more interested in the duck than in Dick and had pulled him over to look at the duck. These strange looking vehicles were quite a novelty after the war and most people had never seen one.

Dick was a heavy drinker. The shipyard had twice sent him to be dried out for about thirty days. He would come back sober, but usually after a month or so he would start back on the booze. I looked forward to coming to work when I knew Dick would be working with us. When he wasn't drinking, he was fun to work with and kept us laughing all night with his fishing stories. He was a natural born storyteller as well as an excellent worker. We always got a lot done when he was with us.

One night at suppertime I asked Dick why he had stopped commercial fishing. He said it was too seasonal—it was either feast or famine. He said that on some trips, they didn't make much after paying for their ice, gas, and groceries. Some fishermen will tell you the only people making money on fishing are the fishing boat manufacturers, banks, insurance companies, and the fish houses.

Dick told me that in the days before LORAN and GPS and the other fancy navigational electronic aids, he had compiled a book of latitude and longitude references. This book listed what species of fish would be at specific locations during spring, summer, fall, and winter. It had taken him a number of years to accumulate all the information. The book enabled the fishermen to go to a specific spot at any time of the year and know what they were going to catch.

He tried to quit fishing on numerous occasions, but the call of the sea was too strong and he always went back. Finally, in desperation, he gave his precious fish book away. He decided that without it, he wouldn't know where the fish were by seasons. That was when he came to work in the shipyard.

The last time he came to work with us, he came a little tipsy. Within an hour, he got worse. Dick was well liked and my boss didn't want to discipline him. He told me to take him, another rigger, our welder and our burner to a part of the yard that was poorly lit. There was a warming shack in the area out of the way. He said to stash Dick in the shack until he sobered up. My crew and I went to work moving some units. Periodically, I would check on Dick.

Just before supper, I went over to the warming shack. A man had his back to me talking to Dick. It was the infamous "Chicken Man" alias "Frank Perdue". He was one of the most hated and feared superintendents in the yard. I ducked behind a stanchion that was in the dark no more than ten feet away and heard the whole conversation. The super asked Dick who he was. Dick mumbled. He then asked him what department he worked in. Dick mumbled. Next question was where he was supposed to be working. Dick mumbled again. By now, the super was really agitated, almost jumping up and down. He asked Dick, "Do you know who I am?" Dick said no. The super said, "My name is Bob Smith." Dick jumped up, almost fell over, and said, "Glad to meet you. My name is Dick Leadgood." He then stuck out his hand to shake hands and the "Chicken Man" stepped aside. Dick fell flat on his face.

Five minutes later, the guards showed up. By then it was suppertime. The guards loaded Dick in their truck and took him away. As soon as they put him in the truck, he rolled down the window and started waving at everybody going to supper.

Dick was once again sent away for another thirty days to dry out. After that, he was placed on the first shift. For a while, I thought about transferring to the first shift to work with good old Dick Leadgood.

For a while, I worked on the third shift (11:00 PM to 7:00 AM). To me, this was the worst shift of all. Some men liked it, especially men who had a day job. How they managed two eight hour shift jobs, I'll never know.

I worked with one man known as "Squeaky", who liked the third shift and usually went to the bar called the Three Sisters (AKA Six Tits) for breakfast at 7:00 AM. One morning, after the end of our shift, he asked me if I wanted to go to breakfast with him. I don't usually like breakfast until 8:30 or so, but I reluctantly agreed to go with him. I was curious as to why he would go to a bar for breakfast as opposed to a coffee shop, and quickly found out. It was the worst breakfast I ever saw or heard of. He ordered one quart of beer and two chocolate donuts, referring to his breakfast as, "The breakfast of champions". I ordered coffee and donuts. To each his own, I guess.

Dogs, Cats, Rats, and Other Critters

We all had to wear picture identification badges at all times in the yard. Quite often, dogs would be seen wandering around the yard at all hours of the day and night. One night, we saw a dog walking our way and my helper said, "Quick, call Security". I said, "Why?". He said, "That dog is not wearing a badge".

Most shipyards have an assortment of cats, rats, and other animals. The yards that I worked at were no exception. Through the years, I saw sea gulls, rats, cats, skunks, opossums, squirrels, raccoons, and a fox. One basin I worked in had a large population of rats. It got so bad and they became so bold that we decided something had to be done. We decided to have a contest between the first and second shifts. Sixteen rat traps were produced and each shift would bait them and set them out at the start of their shift. The first night, we had fourteen by morning. The day shift got nine. The next night, we had sixteen by 10:00 PM. We reset the traps and had six more by midnight. We always got more than the day shift and won the contest hands down. They complained we had an unfair advantage as rats were out more at night. By the end of two weeks, we had cleaned out most of the rats. The only ones left had become shy of the traps or became expert at springing the traps and stealing the bait.

The yard was home to a large population of feral cats of all colors and sizes. They were all wild and most did not have a long life. If you worked in one area for maybe a year, you might see the same cats for half that time and then they would disappear and usually other cats would appear.

Two litters of cats were born beneath the steel floor of one shop I worked in. We pulled up part of this floor to try and get a look at the kittens. What amazed me was that they were just as mean and vicious as their parents. I managed to pick one up with heavy welding gloves on. Talk about having a tiger by the tail! This little month old kitten did more snarling and biting than the adult cats. I quickly dropped it and we put the floor back. It must have been a tough life for these cats with all the rats and possums. Some of the water rats were as big as the cats.

One of the regular shop cats came limping along one day and laid down a distance from us. It was a short haired cat and when I got closer, I could see a big chunk of its neck was missing. The next day we found a big water rat outside our shop, dead. It was a mess and had been completely disemboweled. We figured he and the cat had a fight and he got the cat by the neck. Then, the cat tore up the rat with its back legs and claws. The cat survived and we saw him around the shop months later. We called him "Killer".

We appreciated having the cats around to keep the rats down. Some of the guys brought in cat food for the cats, but I never saw one that became tame. This was probably just as well because some of the guys hated cats and some thought they were "Great White Hunters" (guys who liked to kill anything).

One night I was working with the riggers down in the bottom of a basin. From the basin floor to ground level was 65 feet. At ground level were cranes that lowered material down into the basins. The operator's cab was about 50 feet above ground level and the crane boom stuck up another 40 feet, approximately. The area was well lit from basin floodlights plus floodlights on the cranes. The crane was lowering material down to us. As I was looking up, something fell off the boom on the crane and came sailing down near us. Whatever it was did not fall straight down but rather glided and landed about 50 feet from us near some tool boxes. One of the riggers saw it about the same time I did. We speculated it was probably a bird, maybe injured, or possibly a bat. We started moving tool boxes and there, hiding up against two tool boxes, was a furry little creature. I had on heavy welders' gloves and was able to pick it up. It tried biting me. We got a good look at it and realized it was some type of a squirrel. It was a flying squirrel. They have an extra flap of skin between their front and back legs. It is extended when they "fly" (glide) down to the ground. Their tail serves as a rudder.

For a while, I worked the third shift. My hours were 11 PM to 7 AM. Most animals feed around daybreak and then again around sunset. Between five and seven AM, many animals would appear including what appeared to be tens of thousands of starlings coming out from under the bridge.

One morning, I was working in an open area just at daybreak and saw a dog coming my way. It looked like a medium sized dog, but didn't act like one. I froze as it got closer, hoping to get a better look. It was a beautiful red fox wearing a bushy winter coat with a bushy red tail. It jogged right by me and didn't appear to see me until I let out a hoot. He came about a foot off the ground and took off running and quickly ran behind a building.

Along about this time began the saga of "Louisiana Lou". Louisiana Lou was a dolphin that became trapped in a wet slip at the yard between a ship and a sea wall. A ship by the name of *Louisiana* had sailed out of the yard for sea trials. The previous week two dolphins had been spotted off the stern of the *Louisiana* feeding on pogies. When the *Louisiana* left on trials the dolphins chased the pogies into the wet slip and were still there the following day feeding when the ship came back. The ship was slowly eased into the slip with only about two feet clearance on each side between the hull of the ship and the side of the slip. One of the dolphins swam out, but the other one was so busy that it became trapped by the bow of the ship. When I came into work that night, it was trapped between the bow of the *Louisiana* and the wall of the basin. It had an area to swim in about 130 feet by 75 feet and about 35 feet deep. I remember in the past when similar things had happened and some of the great "hunters" in the yard had killed the dolphins by throwing welding wires and scrap steel at them, literally making a huge pin cushion out of the poor animals. At supper time, I called the local paper and asked them to call the Animal Rescue League and the Department of Natural Resources. They said they would see what they could do.

About two hours later, the State game wardens showed up with reporters and photographers. The yard was forced to post a 24 hour guard on "Louisiana Lou", as the papers soon named her. There were stories in the paper and TV about the incident for about a week. A huge net was brought in and the game wardens tried for about three days to catch the elusive Lou. Finally, she just swam under the ship after about a week and joined her mate who had been waiting in the river for her all week.

Along about this time, there was a severe northeaster with the third highest recorded tide in this area. The water went over the top of the gate at the end of the basin and flooded the basin to a depth of six feet. Everybody's tool boxes were flooded as well as the office. The company said they would pay for anybody's tools that were ruined. We were each given a form to fill out. Each ruined tool was to be listed along with its replacement value. I never knew my co-workers had so many tools. People who had borrowed my level, chalkline, or combination square were listing these amongst their ruined tools. Some people who had never had more than $10 worth of tools suddenly had $200 worth of ruined tools. It got to be a joke as to who could come up with the biggest, most expensive list. The company's insurance paid off, but I do not know anybody who got over $60. The men who complained the loudest about the settlement were the ones who had lost the least.

We were having lunch one day aboard ship when a fin popped up near us in the water and started swimming slowly towards the ship. The fin was flopping back and forth from side to side and stuck up at least one foot. Once again, the "Great White Hunters" started throwing welding wires at the poor critter and it dove under the ship and came back up on the other side. It finally swam slowly away looking like a giant pincushion with all the welding wires in it.

A few years later, part of my crew and I had another encounter with these strange fish. One member of my crew owned a 17 foot Boston Whaler. We decided to go fishing across Massachusetts Bay to Provincetown. If one looks at a map of Massachusetts and follows the long arm of Cape Cod to the end, there sits Provincetown. From Boston to Provincetown by auto is about 150 miles. From our starting point on the South Shore, it's about 20 to 25 miles across open water in Massachusetts Bay. An ambitious trip in a little 17 foot Whaler.

We decided to head across at first light, fish for three to four hours, and head back mid afternoon and go to work that night. We made it across and started bottom fishing in about 90 feet of water one-half mile off the beach. The movie, "Jaws", had just come out and we were talking about it. By this time, we had probably drunk close to a case of beer. I was sitting up in the bow and was starting to think about the long trip back across the open water. The waves were getting bigger and we were talking about hauling up the anchor.

Just then, about 100 feet away, a fin appeared on the surface. This was no little fin. It was about three feet high. One of the guys yelled out, "Jaws!". This monstrous fin was heading for us. I imagined the shark that belonged to this fin was probably longer than our 17 foot Whaler. Talk about pandemonium! Everybody started hauling in their fishing lines. We had about 200 feet of anchor line out. Just then, one of the guys yelled out, "There's another one and then another". We were quickly surrounded by a school of them.

I hauled in that 200 feet of line and had the anchor in the boat before anybody had their fishing lines in. I was standing up in the bow hauling in the anchor when one of those monsters slowly dove under the boat. I got a good look at it. It appeared to be a huge swimming head. At first, I thought that a shark had bitten off the fish's body. Then another one swam close by and we all got a good look at it. It was a head about five feet long and five feet high with a huge two to three foot dorsal fin on top and another just as big underneath. At the end of this huge head was a tail as tall as the head. This fish swam with a strange side to side movement. This caused that massive fin to flop back and forth from side to side. A good swimmer could almost keep up with them. Even though I had only seen one once I was quite sure we were looking at ocean sunfish. They range in size from four to eight feet. The longest one ever caught was 11 feet and weighed close to a ton. We were looking at ones in the 300 to 400 pound range.

Once the excitement died down, we decided to try and catch one. Kenny had some treble (three sided) hooks in his tackle box and put one on and cast out to try to snag one of those fins. After about six casts, he snagged one. Rugrat had the motor going and motored over to it. It quickly snapped the line. Brownie had heavier line on his pole and he snagged one. I vacated the bow and Kenny and Brownie got up into the bow and reeled him in. I thought it was way too big to bring into our little boat, but they were determined. We got into the stern to make the bow more buoyant and they started wrestling with this huge headed giant. Kenny tried to get his arms around it and Brownie tried to get the tail. I thought we were going to sink. Years ago, Boston Whaler showed a Whaler cut in half with a chain saw. It still floated like a cork. I thought about this ad and wondered if we would ever get across the bay with this monster in the boat.

As I watched this struggle from the stern, I noticed the fish had a huge eye, probably about three to four inches in diameter. Its eye was focused on its chief tormentor, Kenny. All of a sudden, Kenny was hit square in the face by a torrent of water not unlike a fire hose. The sunfish had pumped a gusher of water out of his gills. Kenny dropped him like a hot potato and we all got a big laugh at Kenny's expense. We snagged a couple more and brought them to the boat for a look. This was one of those fish stories that you had to be there to believe.

Shortly after, we headed across the bay and all agreed we would go to work that night. That night, when I got to work, three of the best shipfitters on my crew never showed up.

The crew I worked with was a great bunch of guys and we had a lot of fun together in and out of work. About ten of us worked together for a period of about five years. Twice a year, we would go salt water fishing. Every spring and fall we would go to a local boat livery and rent two 16 foot skiffs with outboard motors. Two men sat in the middle, one in the bow, and one in the stern. The area that we fished is called Quincy Bay and reputedly has the best flounder fishing on the east coast.

There are about four boat liveries in the area and in the spring and fall, reservations must be made weeks in advance to get a boat. One memorable trip in particular stands out in my mind. We all met at the boat livery about 7 AM and loaded the boats. Pete the Polack arrived already loaded. He used to drive about 45 miles to get there and must have started drinking at the crack of dawn. All the food, bait, tackle boxes, foul weather gear, and fishing poles were put in the boats. The boats were so loaded there was no room for the beer. We had a discussion and couldn't make up our minds if we should leave Pete the Polack ashore or our beer. Somehow or other, we squeezed everything in including the beer and Pete. Somebody made the remark that the quicker we drank the beer and jettisoned the cans, the more room we would have. Everybody agreed to this and all hands fell to this task.

Pete the Polack said that he had never seen a congo eel or skate and if anybody caught one or both of them he would like to see them. We motored out into the bay and started fishing. We anchored a mile from the boat livery. The fish were not biting too good so we lifted anchor and moved about two miles away from Pete's boat and anchored behind an island. We caught lots of flounder, four crabs, a skate, and a congo eel for Pete the Polack. Usually, if we caught these types of fish we fed them to the seagulls as they were considered trash fish.

After about five hours of fishing, we started getting low on bait and decided to check out Pete the Polack's boat and see if they had any bait to spare. We hauled in the anchor, started the engine, and motored over to where we had left them. By this time, there were about fifty skiffs fishing this one area and we had a hard time finding Pete's boat. We finally found Pete's boat by a trail of beer cans floating down the bay. When we got close to their boat, Pete yelled over and wanted to know if we had any beer left. He said they were getting low on beer and we asked him if they had any bait left. They had plenty of bait left. It seems they were doing more drinking than fishing. The man up in the bow of their boat had passed out and he was sleeping wedged into the bow. This same man always took the bow of the boat. He used to sit right up in the bow with both arms draped over the sides like he was holding the boat together. The only time he changed this position was when he would light a cigarette or drink a beer. Now he was collapsed on the seat and half on the floor. The bow did not look right without him there and we commented on whether the boat would stay together without him hugging the bow. We made the exchange of bait and beer and dropped anchor nearby.

About an hour later it was agreed we should start back to the boat livery. We hauled in the anchor and started the motor. We went over to Pete's boat and asked him if they were coming in. Brownie, one of the men on our boat, had grabbed the Congo eel and yelled to Pete and asked him if he still wanted to see a Congo eel. Pete said yes, did we catch one. He had no sooner got the words out of his mouth when Brownie threw the Congo eel at him and it hit him square in the mouth. We gunned the motor and steered in a circle around their anchored boat. As we came around again, Brownie threw the skate at Pete and scored another direct hit. Pete was furious. Brownie yelled over at him, "I thought you wanted to see a congo eel and a skate". Pete hauled his anchor, started his motor, and came after us. When they got just off our stern, Brownie started bombarding them with empty beer cans. They started throwing them back at us. We were moving right along and every can they threw at us would just about make it to our boat and then the wind would catch it and it would end up blowing back at them. One of the men in Pete's boat was a very serious fisherman and had been mad all day at Pete because of all the drinking. One of the cans Pete threw drifted back and hit him in the face. He grabbed Pete's hat and threw it overboard. Pete grabbed his Thermos and threw it overboard. This started to get serious and we were wondering if we might have to go back and pull the both of them out of the water. They finally quieted down.

Next thing we knew, they had turned their boat around and went motoring off for the Thermos and the hat. We proceeded on to the boat livery and a short time later, they all showed up much subdued and quiet. Pete got out of his boat and headed for the nearest bar. He came back a short time later even drunker and fell off the pier. We had our fish cleaned, divided them up, and everybody went home. I thought for a while we might have to drive Pete the Polack home but he eventually sobered up. I think falling off the pier into the cold water helped.

At certain times of the year, different types of fish came into the bay in large numbers. Some of the men kept drop lines in their toolboxes for fishing. Some ardent fishermen would tie a dropline to the pier and periodically check it during the day. Bottom fishing would usually yield an assortment of flounders, perch, eels, and many crabs. When the bait fish moved up the bay, huge schools of blue-fish would follow them. At times when they were feeding the water would churn up and fins of the bluefish could be seen on the surface. Bluefish are voracious feeders and when they are in a feeding frenzy, they have been known to attack humans. A bluefish will average about 7–8 pounds, but 14 pounds is not uncommon. They are considered to be a game fish and many are taken on rod and reel. A bluefish when brought aboard a boat will snap at everything in sight. Most experienced bluefish fishermen carry a small club on their boat. Usually before the hook is removed, a blues fisherman will hit the blue on the head repeatedly before attempting to remove the hook.

About the same time the blues arrive, striped bass come up the coast. A striper is the favorite sport fish of most saltwater fishermen in this area. One of my co-workers was an ardent blue and bass fisherman. When the bass or blues were in season, he would fish every night at suppertime. He brought in a fold up casting rod and kept it in his tool box with an assortment of plugs and lures. He did not have much luck, but spent every supper time casting into the bay. Patience finally paid off and one supper time he caught a 32 pound striped bass. The company guards got quite a shock at quitting time. We walked out the gate together, I with my lunchbox and him with a 32 pound bass over his shoulder. The guards were always on the lookout for somebody trying to steal company property. This fish was definitely not company property.

Before a ship was floated out, the building basin would be flooded. After the basin was flooded, the gate at the end of the basin was lowered and the ship would then be towed out of the basin by tugs. When the ship left the basin, the gate would be raised. When the gate was raised, the pumps were turned on and the basin was pumped dry. Sometimes, after a basin was pumped dry, thousands of smelt were left high and dry on the basin floor.

The smelt ran at certain predictable times of the year. They are highly prized as a food fish. When they are running, many fishermen spend a lot of time pursuing them. I have seen men go down into the basin and come out with a hundred pounds or more of smelt.

Thomas W. Lawson, the world's only seven masted schooner

Launched in Quincy in 1902. Twenty thousand people attended the launching,

Above: The family store with the author's
mother, Edith. (Note band on telephone
pole: this was Pudgy's bus stop.)
Below: Pudgy, the Wonder Dog, begging for donuts.

U.S.S. Wasp, commissioned in 1943.
She replaced the Quincy-built
Wasp which was sunk in 1942.

U.S.S. Lexington (The Blue Ghost), presently
a museum ship in Corpus Christi, Texas. She
was launched in 1943 and replaced the
Quincy-built Lexington which was sunk in 1942.

(US Navy photo)

Above: U.S.S. Massachusetts, presently a museum ship in Fall River, Massachusetts.
Below: The Rivadavia, built for the Argentine Navy in 1914.
She was decommissioned in the 1940s and scrapped in 1956.

U.S.S. Salem, underway.

U.S.S. Salem in Venice, Italy. (She is presently a museum ship at the Fore River Shipyard in Quincy, Massachusetts).

Above: The Constitution. The ocean liner Independence and her sister ship,
Constitution were both launched in 1951 for American Export Lines. They were built for the New York
to Mediterranean runs in the days when transatlantic cruises were still popular. After
many years operating in the Hawaiian Islands as America's only American registered cruise ships,
the decision was made to retire the Constitution. In 1997 she was being towed and was lost.

Below: The Manhattan, weighing in at 106,000 tons,
she was the world's heaviest ship when commissioned in 1962.

The Nuclear Powered Navy. U.S.S. Enterprise,
U.S.S. Long Beach and U.S.S. Bainbridge.
The Long Beach and the Bainbridge were built in Quincy.

Above: Watson's bridge, ca. 1902. Built by the yard to
accommodate their new cruiser, the Des Moines.
Below: The U.S.S. Whale, delivered in 1968.

Above: Dr. Lykes (Sea-bee).
Below: The elevator on the stern: the largest ever installed on any ship, including super aircraft carriers.

Above and below: navy oiler, U.S.S. Kalamazoo, last
ship launched "down the ways" in Quincy in 1971.

The Goliath crane lowering the
deck house onto a LNG in a basin.

A partial view of the Fore River Shipyard with 3 LNGs (two in the water and one in a basin) prior to launching.

Above: the barge, Hercules, carrying a
120 foot sphere for the LNG Aquarius.
Below: LNG Aquarius.

2nd LT John P. Bobo passing through
the Fore River drawbridge.

Coffee Breaks, Card Games and Safety

We had many roamers who would spend the better part of their shift wandering around the yard talking and goofing off. Sometimes, you wondered how the ships ever got built. Fortunately, there was a dedicated core of workers who always did their work.

Everybody always complained about the union and how poor it was; however, it was strong enough to protect all the goof-offs from being fired. We used to say a man had to be completely useless to get fired. The union would battle the company all the way when the company tried to fire somebody for an infraction of the rules. About the only thing they could fire a person for was stealing and fighting.

There were thieves among us who had devious ways of getting material out of the yard. Years ago, many boat and utility trailers were built in the yard. In the morning, you would drive your car in with trailer wheels and an axle in your trunk. At night, you would drive your car out with your new trailer trailing behind. Valuable material was taken out in the trunks of cars. The bosses were reputed to be the biggest thieves of all.

The yard put a stop to all this by banning cars in the yard. One night we were playing softball next to the yard, the field being lit by the yard floodlights. Adjacent to the ball field was a private parking lot. Along the fence there were some bushes and parked cars. A car drove into the parking lot and two men got out and opened the trunk. They loaded many hundred pounds of lead and copper into the trunk. When they were done, two yard policemen got out of an "empty" car parked by the fence and arrested them.

There were many junk collectors in the yard who would steal any copper, brass, aluminum, lead, or nickel scrap or bolts they could lay their hands on. One hot summer day one of these junkies passed out going through the gate at quitting time. The guards carried him into the guard shack. He appeared to be very heavy. Wrapped around his body was about 120 pounds of copper wire. He was fired.

We had a welder working in our area called "Alabama". He was a kleptoma-niac. He never stole anything expensive but every afternoon he would take some-thing home. His loot was usually toilet paper, paper towels, light bulbs, Ajax, etc. One day, he was caught by the guards at the gate with an unopened can of Ajax. The company gave him five days off without pay. The rumor was they would have fired him if he had not worked there for many years. We all got a big laugh out of this incident. Almost getting fired for stealing a can of Ajax!

The company had a strange way of dealing with excessive absenteeism. Many people did not put in a forty hour week. It was permissible to take about a day and a half off a month. Anything more than that called for disciplinary action by management. First offense would be a verbal warning. Second offense would be a written warning. Third offense, three days off without pay. Many employees would try to get the three days off so it would make a long weekend. The next offense called for five days off without pay. If this happened again in a six month period, the employee could be fired. Many employees got this three day or five day vacation and loved it. I could never see the logic in this kind of punishment. I have seen people who were going on vacation try to get an extra three or five days off by this method.

The yard had many employees who either had a side job or sold merchandise for extra income. If you wanted to have anything done on your car or house there was someone who knew someone who did that type of work. Many items were offered for sale every day, some of them stolen. You could buy anything from ten pounds of veal to an outboard motor, all stolen and about half price. Illegal items and services were also offered. You could buy any kind of drugs or firearms; even have somebody's car or house vandalized right down to having someone's legs broken. These services were a little harder to find but were offered.

The government had placed many hard core unemployed in the yard and was picking up the tab for their pay. Many of them were ex-convicts and felons. Some of them were impossible to rehabilitate and used the yard as a store for their ille-gal drugs and other assorted activities including bookmaking. Lots of them were minorities and the first line bosses despised this group. Not because they were minorities but because the company would not let their bosses discipline them. The government said they had to have so many minorities in each trade. A lot of them were worthless and had no intention of working but the company would not fire them because they had to keep their quotas of minorities. This was very discouraging for the bosses as it made for bad morale amongst the other workers. If these people could get away with murder why not everybody?

Many of them were promoted into management positions because the government said a certain percentage of them had to be at management level, one of the bad parts of having government contracts. If a man is not willing to work he should be fired. There were instances when minorities were promoted into higher paying positions because they were minorities. This was done at the expense of someone better qualified but who was not a minority. This created many bad feelings and took away a man's incentive to do good work and try and get ahead in the company. Some of these people promoted into these positions could barely speak English and did not know the trade they were put in charge of. Still, the ships were built and delivered on time.

The word was put out one day that the company photographer would be up on the high side taking pictures. This was a mammoth skeletal structure, 185 feet high, which housed the overhead cranes. We thought his purpose was to take pictures of men goofing off. Every trade in the yard wore different color hats and this was how you knew what trade a man worked for. When we spotted the cameraman with his projector, we all took off our hats and stopped working. A couple of men gave him the finger and one man even dropped his drawers and mooned the projector. So much for the cameraman and that idea to frighten the workers into more productivity.

One cold day down in the hold of a partially completed ship, we built a fire in a 55 gallon barrel. Somebody threw a few oil soaked planks in and a short time later we had the smokiest fire imaginable. The ship was smoking so bad that the Fire Department was called. They thought the whole ship was on fire.

For many years the yard had an incentive system on government ships. The system worked this way: an estimator would figure a particular job would take, say, 100 hours. A man would do the job and if he did it in less than 100 hours he would be paid a bonus on all hours under 100. The estimated hours allotted were usually generous for most jobs. In this way, a worker could sometimes make two weeks pay in only forty hours. This was an incentive plan where the men made extra money for working hard and the government got ships quickly and at a reduced cost.

A very serious abuse of the incentive system occurred with the welders. They made their incentive pay based on the quantity of weld they installed, measured both linearly and by the cross-section. On fillet joints, which connected a perpendicular plate to a horizontal plate, the cross section weld usually required five to six passes of weld to complete the joint. Instead of using this method, an unscrupulous welder would lay a staging bolt into the open joint and cover it with two passes of weld. In this way, he could complete the job in one-third of the time and, therefore, be entitled to a bonus equal to three times his normal weld. This practice was called "slugging" and was extremely dangerous as it weakened the welded joint to the extent that it would crack under stress and eventually fail. A vessel going to war is not a place for poor workmanship.

On the tanker, *Manhattan*, slugging was discovered by x-ray of critical structural welds. This resulted in the firing of a number of welders and welding supervision.

Another example of slugging occurred when, during the dismantling of overhead steel structures used to support overhead cranes, it was discovered that a number of these welds had been slugged when the structures was erected years earlier. Why those welds never failed, nobody knows.

One of the problems with a union shop is that a hard worker is not paid any more for his work than a lazy one. This was one of the great things about contract jobs. On most contract jobs, welders were paid by the foot. The only problem was it encouraged shoddy workmanship and shortcuts. If a compartment called for five coats of paint, in some cases, it would only get four or three. A welder welding up a seam or butt would insert scrap steel or welding wires in seams or butts. This would greatly speed up his work. This got to be quite a disgrace and was probably one of the reasons contract jobs were abolished. A lot of workmen made big money under this system, though, and many fine ships were turned out in record time.

The Federal government says the only more dangerous job than working in shipyards is working in the mining industry. I believe this wholeheartedly. You name it for bad working conditions—a shipyard has it. Through the years this writer has worked at four of them and they are all about the same. Dust, dirt, air pollution, grease, oil, fires, cold, rain, snow, sleet, hail, wind, heat, humidity—you name it, a shipyard has it. It's a wonder that they don't have more fatal accidents than they do with the poor working conditions. In one five year period, I can remember six people losing their lives in one particular shipyard and scores more being permanently disabled from crippling injuries. Still, with all the dangers, the shipyard was a very interesting and funny place to work.

A co-worker's wife used to bake delicious pies, pastries, and other assorted goodies. At lunch time one day, he finished his sandwiches and couldn't find any dessert. That night he asked his wife about it. She said she had put pie in his lunch box. The next day, the same thing happened again. He used to leave his lunch in the same place every day, but the next day, he took it with him to his job. At lunch time, the dessert was missing again. For the rest of the week he watched it like a hawk and the dessert still disappeared every day. One of his wife's specialties was toll house cookies, so he asked her to put a whole package of ex-lax in the cookies. The following afternoon, his helper who worked with him every day visited the toilet five times with the runs. The next day he had a new helper and dessert at lunch time.

Frequently, a worker's lunch would disappear in the morning. Somebody would be broke and hungry and steal lunches. The worst offenders were the seagulls. If you left a sandwich or a brown paper bag in the open, it would disappear nine times out of ten. We would never warn new men about this and used to get a laugh when a gull would fly off with someone's lunch.

Drinking was always a problem at shipyards. Even more so in the winter time. Many men would bring in a pint to help ward off the cold. Brandy was a favorite of most workers. After one especially cold night, we found raspberry, ginger, apricot, peach, blackberry, and other assorted brandy bottles in a trash barrel.

One day, my partner came into work partially drunk. My boss put myself and him in a tank aboard ship to hide him. This tank was an oil storage tank on an 80,000 ton tanker. The only access to this tank was down a vertical sixty foot ladder. Its dimensions were approximately 110 feet wide by 120 feet long. Down the centerline of the tank was a swash bulkhead with 18 inch to 36 inch holes in it. A bulkhead of this type is to stop the oil from moving about in the tank in a rough sea. By supper time, my partner had sobered up enough to help us. The job we were doing consisted of putting reinforcing brackets on longitudinals connected to frames. After supper, we started back working on the brackets. By 9:00 PM my partner appeared to be getting drunk again. By 10:00 PM there was no doubt of it. By 11:00 PM he had passed out in the bottom of the tank. We were due to finish up our shift at 12:00 AM and I knew he would be in no condition to walk by then. Our boss was a reasonable person who I knew would not discipline my partner so I climbed out of the tank and went to the office and told him about my partner.

At first, he was going to get First Aid and have the medics haul him out with a sling stretcher. Then he decided they would have to turn in a report to management and the man would probably be suspended by the company. We decided to try and haul him out by ourselves. He was not a big man, probably about 5 feet 6 inches and 110 pounds. We stood him up, put a rope sling under his armpits, and tied it over my shoulders. We carried him over to the sixty foot ladder and I started up with him more or less tied to my shoulders. My boss climbed up behind us and more or less pushed him up to take some of the weight. Now, 110 pounds may not sound like much but when it is dead weight hanging it feels like 300 pounds. After about fifteen minutes of pushing and pulling, we got him to the main deck. At 1135, we dumped him into a six foot long stainless steel sink in a men's room and turned on the cold water full blast. By midnight, he was in good enough shape to walk out the gate with just a little help from me.

The following day, I worked in the same tank with a different partner. It didn't take long to figure out what had happened. At supper time, my partner of the previous night had gone to a liquor store and bought a pint of brandy. Tucked behind a steel T beam was an empty pint brandy bottle, his favorite liquor.

For a long time we had played cards every night at supper time. There was always four players and three or more kibitzers. We had a nice little room aboard ship and had fixed it up with lights, a table, chairs, even a heater. Now this was all right until we started taking 45 minutes for supper and before long, an hour or more. We always played whist but the games got longer and longer. Our boss warned us and said we were going to get into big trouble if we continued playing after supper every night. We had the perfect solution for that. We started playing one half hour early. This worked out fine for about two weeks until our boss realized seven or eight men were missing every night before supper. Our boss caught us the following night and told us we would all get a chit if he caught us again. Three of these chits in a six month period were grounds for dismissal, so you had to be careful.

The following night about five minutes before supper there was a knock on the door and everybody froze. We had a lock on the door but there was only one way in or out. The boss said open the door. Still nobody moved. Finally he said he would get the company security guards. We reluctantly opened it and he stormed in with chit book in his hand. We had put the cards away but he knew we had been playing. He asked us what we had been playing. Somebody said "Kitty Whist". Just then the supper whistle blew. I asked him if he wanted to sit in a hand. Much to my surprise he sat down and played. Needless to say, he put his chit book away. He did warn us, though. No more chances.

So, we decided we needed a new area for our nightly card game. It was further agreed we also should play at a different time. The ships we were working on then were landing ship docks (LSDs). They were about 535 feet long with about an 85 foot beam and about 18,000 tons. These ships were quite unique. They had a conventional bow and their profile looked like a conventional ship but the stern had a huge gate that swung down under water. The whole mid section of the ship from 100 feet aft of the bow back to the stern gate was hollow. Tanks in the bilge of the ship were flooded and the ship would partially submerge. The stern gate would lower and landing craft or a small ship would be floated out the stern of the ship. The stern gate would then be raised, the tanks pumped out and the ship would rise back up to its normal waterline. The Navy also used these ships in areas of the world to repair ships where they did not have dry dock facilities. They were completely equipped with a machine shop and many similar shops.

Mounted near the stern, port and starboard, were two large 75 ton cranes. We decided the cab of one of these cranes would be a good place for our nightly card games. They were in an out of the way place and hard to get to. The following night about a half hour before supper, we opened the cab door and climbed into the room. We had a great came of cards and decided to leave to go back to work shortly after the supper whistle blew. I tried the door and it would not open. Somebody else tried it with the same result. The lock was jammed. Then everybody tried it but it wouldn't budge.

We all looked around for another way out. The only alternative appeared to be windows on the side of the cab. We opened one and looked out. It was about a forty foot drop down to the main deck. Somebody noticed there was a hole where the hoist cable for the crane passed through the front of the cab. My card partner climbed out and down the structure on the front of the crane. One slip and he would have fallen thirty-five feet to the main deck. We all made it and got back to work about a half hour after supper. All in all, a great card came at the shipyard. The following night we all played cards back at the old stand.

The third shift hours were from 11 PM to 7 AM. Usually people on this shift stopped work for supper at 3 AM. A few of them never went back to work. On board a partially completed ship, the only heat would be in the engine room. Everybody would eat supper here. Many third shift employees worked day jobs so by 3 AM they would be tired. One night at supper time, there were about forty yard birds gathered down the engine room. By 4 AM this number had swelled to about sixty. On the engine room floor, three card games were being played and about twenty men were curled up near heaters, sleeping. It was very cold, down below zero, and nobody was working. It was understood by everyone on this shift that you would be on your assigned job by 6 AM when the first shift supervisors would start coming into work. This particular night, nobody went back to work after supper because of the weather.

Shortly after 6 AM, a first shift superintendent entered the engine room. There were the card games and the people lying around sleeping. It looked like a Civil War battlefield with bodies everywhere. Somebody yelled and everybody started running anywhere there was an exit. I was perched up on top of a boiler out of sight watching the whole show. And what a show! The men who did not wake up were given chits and some of them were suspended. Gambling was strictly taboo and two of the card players were caught with money on the table. They were fired. After that, the third shift superintendent was transferred onto the day shift.

One day, a co-worker decided he was going home early. He hopped the fence and started thumbing a ride. Along came the superintendent of his department who stopped to give him a ride. He asked him why he was not at work and the man said he had taken the whole day off. The following day, the superintendent asked his boss about this and the boss said the man had been at work all day. The worker got a chit and the boss got a reprimand placed in his file.

This worker was always getting into one jam or another. He had a girlfriend in work and a wife at home. He was not discreet about this extramarital affair and carried on quite openly with his girlfriend. Every midnight, his practice was to stop for a drink or two at a local bar after work. When he got to the bar one night, there was a bigger than usual crowd gathered around the floor. He elbowed his way up to the front and there two girls were fighting on the floor really going at it. He commented to one of the spectators this was great! A second later, he realized it was his wife and his girlfriend. A friend of mine later told me he did not know what to do. He decided to just keep watching at a discreet distance and finally left before the two fighters spotted him.

The yard was an enormous place. Roughly about a mile by a mile and a half. Some workers liked to wander and roam. It used to be said that if you carried a blueprint under your arm, you could wander at will over the whole place. This was probably true to some extent because I have been stopped by a boss and asked where I was going on many occasions. I was never asked when I had a blueprint under my arm. Reading blueprints aboard ship was not difficult once you learned how. Out in the yard, it was a completely different story. The vast majority of the units were built upside down for the sake of convenience. The blueprints were all right side up and the units were all upside down. This made it easier to build the units but made it difficult to read the blueprints. A person had to have the ability to read the plans and then be able to reverse them in his mind so he could figure out how the various bulkheads, decks, and beams fit together. Sometimes this was easy, but sometimes it was very difficult. In most cases, the units on the port side were identical to ones on the starboard but plans would be only drawn for one side. So, if you were working on a port unit and had starboard plans, it really got very complicated.

One night we were working with the crane and riggers assembling a unit. We built the whole unit. It measured about 22 feet by 40 feet and about 10 feet high. Its weight was 27 tons. Two pieces did not fit together right. We studied the plans thoroughly and finally decided the pieces had been made wrong originally. Still something did not look right. We called the boss over. He studied the unit and the plan. After a lot of measurements and discussions, he came to the same conclusion as we did that the two pieces had been built wrong. The following day when we came into work, the day shift told us we had built the whole unit backwards. They all had a good laugh at our expense. The first shift had to get the crane and completely disassemble the unit and put it back together right. There was always a lot of rivalry between the two shifts and they loved when we made a mistake, especially a big one like this.

The cranes in this part of the yard were all 50 tonners with the exception of one 75 tonner. The newest one was built in the late 1950s; the oldest in the 1920s. They broke down frequently. In one six month period, three different booms on these cranes fell. This was blamed on the crane operation. Luckily, no one was hurt when these booms fell. This was very fortunate as these booms were 100 feet long and weighed many tons each. The fact that no one was hurt was really amazing as all three of them fell during the first shift. Usually at this time of day there would be over 100 people working in the area. When one of the booms fell, the outward 20 feet of the boom was badly damaged. We worked all weekend building new pieces for it. The tip of the boom is called the jib. The surveyors came down and stretched piano wire between two uprights and gave us very precise measurements to hold when we reassembled the jib to the undamaged part of the boom. A very elaborate cradle was built to hold the boom and jib as they were being reassembled. Then the surveyors gave us more measurements to hold and the repaired jib was picked up by another crane and was supposed to be lowered gently into place on the new cradle. The crane operator brought the repaired jib down on to the cradle too fast and knocked down the cradle and the piano wires that we were going to measure off. By this time, it was 4 AM and the surveyors had gone home. The boss had also gone and the boom was supposed to be ready for the welders in the morning. We didn't know what to do at this stage so we just said the heck with it and had the crane pick up the boom, wedged it up to its approximate location and eyeballed it. It looked level and true as best as we could see. We tack welded it together and went home.

The welding engineer had been down earlier in the day and told the welders how to weld it when it was ready for welding. On all repaired parts of the boom, there were four spots that could be welded. The engineer only wanted two of these spots welded that could be welded. Welded in this way, the boom would be able to flex and twist slightly when a load was put on it. When I came in the following afternoon, the boom was all welded up and ready to be hoisted back up onto the crane it had fallen from. If a boom is welded up solid, it will not flex and it will fail if not able to flex. This is much the same as a tree that bends in the wind. A tree that will not bend will break. Similar to a tall building that is designed so that it will sway in very windy weather. If it did not sway, it would collapse. When I checked out the boom, it had been welded up solid at all four junctions on every repaired part. For many months later, I would not go near that crane when it had a heavy load on it.

Saturday night when we were working on the boom, the boss said he was going out for pizza. He said anybody who wanted a pizza should give him the money. There were twelve of us plus the boss. Everybody ordered one. About two hours later, he came back with the pizza and told us to go into the office two at a time to eat the pizza. We said the heck with that, who wants cold pizza. So we all trooped into the office and ate our pizza. About fifteen minutes later, I was putting the last piece into my mouth when the boss came into the office. He started looking through the pizza boxes and finally asked where his pizza was. I asked him how many pizzas he had bought and he said twelve. I told him he forgot to include himself in the order. Boy, was he mad! Somebody took pity on him and gave him a peanut butter sandwich. He was still mumbling about the pizza an hour later and said that would be the last time he went out for pizzas.

A short time later, we were doing a repair job on a damaged tanker. Damaged units were brought to our area and we cut the damaged parts out and replaced them with new steel. One unit was brought in that weighed 89 tons. We completely rebuilt the unit and even put in some heavier steel and reinforcing according to the plan for the unit. A week later, it was all welded up and ready to go. Two fifty ton cranes were hooked on it and started lifting. One end came off the cradle but the other end would not budge. A discussion was held amongst the bosses. They decided to try and pick it up another way. The wires on the cranes were hooked up to another place on the unit and the cranes tried picking it up again. One end came off the cradle and the other end still would not budge. An engineer and the head of the department were called in from their homes. Many other methods were tried to no avail. About 11:00 PM the decision was made to cut the unit in two and weld it back together on the ship. This unit was top priority so I was asked to work a double shift on it until 7:00 Sunday morning. At first I said no because I was slated to work Sunday night from 3:30 to midnight. Suddenly I realized that after midnight I would be on double time. This made me change my mind. On that weekend I made 44 hours pay. Saturdays were paid at the rate of time and one half and Sundays, double time. It made for a nice check and Uncle Sam loved the deductions.

When they finally got the unit on the ship and weighed it, it weighed in at 123 tons. All told, about 34 tons more than the engineer had figured. If the cranes had been able to pick it up, we might have had to work overtime rebuilding two more booms.

When it was time for union elections, the shipyard would be covered by handbills and handwritten campaign slogans in every prominent area. The workers even started putting campaign stickers on their hardhats. The hats were supplied by the company. The company said there would be no political slogans on hats. They did not mind people putting their own names on their hardhats but some people went to extremes and looked like walking billboards. The new rule about political slogans seemed to be strictly carried out. Other men liked to put comical saying on their hats. Stickers on some hats would say "Low Bridge" or "Danger 440 volts" or "Hazardous area" or "Yogi Bear". The wearing of hard hats was strictly enforced at all times and saved many a person from serious injury.

Weather was always a problem and the company lost production time because of this. When it rained, they would try to find indoor work for us. Sometimes, it got so hot that you could literally fry an egg on the steel. If you could not find a shady area to work it was murder. It would be an excellent place for an overweight person to work. They could literally sweat off pounds in the intense heat. When it snowed, you were handed a shovel and told to shovel snow. If this was not your idea of work, you were sent home without pay. If it snowed early in the season, the snow would freeze on the steel. Sometimes, it would take weeks to melt.

The plate yard covered over an acre and had about eighty stacks of steel. These were all arranged in neat rows and stacked sandwich style, one on top of another. One stack would have plates of all one thickness, say 1/4 inch; the next stack, 3/8 inch, and so on right up to plates of one and 1/4 inch thick. The plates were usually about 8 to 10 feet wide and 30 to 40 feet long. Some of the stacks were 10 feet high. We used to be able to figure out roughly how much more work the yard had on the books by the height of the stacks of steel. When snowed, the company would send a big crew of men to shovel the snow off these plates. The cranes in the plate yard were all equipped with magnets, but if the plates got covered with ice or snow, the magnets would not work.

One cold afternoon it started snowing heavily and they sent a large gang to the plate yard. It snowed so hard, one to two inches an hour, that by the time you got from one end to the other shoveling, the end you started on would be covered with snow again. Many men gave up and went home. A few of us stayed and worked on. We had a boss that was a real pusher. Every time somebody stopped to get dried out or warm, he would harass them into going back to work.

At midnight, the shift changed and they asked us if we wanted to work overtime till 7:00 AM. At midnight, we would be paid time and one half for overtime. It was still snowing hard, but a few men agreed to stay. At midnight, another crew was sent over to help us. These were all regular third shift workers. The boss we had gone home and a third shift boss took over. A friend of mine disappeared about 11 PM and I thought he went home. We worked all night and the snow finally let up early in the morning. About 6:15 AM, my friend that I thought went home showed up and started shoveling with me. By 7 AM we had all the stacks shoveled off. Shortly thereafter, the boss came around to pass out the time cards. He didn't know us and had to ask our names so he could give us our time cards. When he gave my friend his card, he looked at him rather strangely and said, "Where were you working tonight?" My friend replied, "I shoveled those two plates down the corner and these two here." The boss didn't know whether to believe him or not. He couldn't prove otherwise as he had spent most of the night in the office. After he left, I said to my friend, "I thought you went home." He replied, "About 11 PM I was so tired and wet I went into the lunch room to dry out. The boss came in and kicked me out. After that I shoveled for a short time and then went up to the fourth floor ladies room. It was nice and warm and there was a couch in there. I fell asleep and woke up at 5:15 AM". We stayed outside and shoveled most of the night and he slept! We both got paid the same amount. Oh, well. I wish I had done the same thing.

One night, we were shoveling the same area and the boss sent someone out to get Chinese food. After it arrived, we all went into the office and ate. Afterwards, the boss took out a goatskin wine bag. He passed it around. One man shoveling with us loved his booze. Didn't matter what it was as long as it was alcohol. The wine bag was the type that you hold in two hands and squeeze a stream of wine into your mouth. It is usually held about 6 inches from the mouth. John took the bag and tried it. It went every place but into his mouth. He tried it again. The second time, he hit the target. The man next to him reached for the bag for his turn. John said, "One more time. I'm just beginning to get the hang of this." The third time, he drank about a glassful. Again the man next to him reached for the wine bag. John said, "I think I've got it now," and put the bag up again and drank another glassful. By this time, the boss was wondering if John was going to leave any wine for him. He finally surrendered the bag and by the time it got back to the boss, it was empty. He called us a bunch of ungrateful winos and told us to go back to work shoveling. When we got back to the plate yard, John commented on how much warmer it was. It was 1:30 AM and didn't feel any warmer to me.

Sometimes when we came into work on the second shift, we would get weather passes for hard rain, snow, or sleet. Never for the cold! If the company gave you a weather pass before four hours had elapsed on your shift, you were paid for the whole four hours. The trick was to get a weather pass as soon as possible. Usually, the company would find some dry work or make us hang around waiting for the weather to clear. Once in a while, we would get a weather pass within an hour of the start of our shift. On one memorable occasion, on the second shift I saw my boss at 3:15. Our starting time was 3:30 PM. By 3:20 he had signed my time card for a weather pass. I was out of the parking lot and on my way home when the 3:30 whistle blew. Not bad! I was home before 4:00 PM with four hours pay. Things like this did not happen very often. Sometimes they would just make us hang around till 7:30 PM suppertime and if the weather still had not cleared, they would send us home.

Tool boxes were always being moved around the yard as crews were shifted from one ship or area to another. Sometimes we would be assigned to a new work area and our tool boxes would not arrive till the next day, so in the meantime, we would usually be assigned to an unsavory job called "picking up scrap". Many men thought this was below their dignity. They considered themselves craftsmen and picking up scrap was beneath them. Usually, we could either pick up scrap or go home. Not any old scrap but scrap that was peculiar to your trade. In our case, this consisted of welding wire and steel. Not any steel, but steel particular to our trade. Another job was rolling up welding lines. Not any welding lines, but only the thin lines that we used. The heavy lines belonged to the welders and it was their job to pick up their lines. Sometimes, men would spend more time deciding what to pick up than actually picking up.

One night, I came into work and my tool box had disappeared. I couldn't work without tools, so the boss gave me permission to see if I could find it. I looked around and finally ended up over in the next building basin. After checking out many boxes, I found my own. The padlock was still intact and I made arrangements with the riggers to have a crane ship it back to where I was.

Three days later it was gone again. I went over to the next basin and sure enough, there it was. My padlock had been cut off and there was a new one on it. Again, I made arrangements to have it shipped back. After the crane set it down, I had a burner cut the padlock off. A painter gave me some bright blue paint. After painting it, I installed a new padlock. The following night when I came into work the boss told us to stack up our tool boxes as we were being transferred to another area. My tool box had disappeared again. I went over to the next basin to the usual place, but it was not there. This was getting to be a pain in the neck. After looking around, I found it in a warming shack. The crane picked it up and we moved to our new area. I thought this would be the end of the disappearing tool box. The area that we went to work in was about one half mile away from where we had last worked. A few months later, a man transferred onto our crew. That afternoon, I was getting tools out of my box and he came over and asked me where I had gotten the tool box from. I told him I had it for over a year. He said he had found it in a basin and somebody kept stealing it from him and had even cut his lock off and painted it. I replied that I had originally drawn it out of the tool room. We went round and round like this and he finally said he had been on the first shift and had never seen anybody near the box. He figured the owner had quit the yard and left the box behind. He was on the first shift then and I was on the second. Our paths never crossed. He finally agreed that it was my box and I gave him his tools that were still in it. We became good friends and had a good laugh over the wandering tool box.

The workers at one time had all worn the same color hats with each department's number printed on the hats. The company then changed this and had different color hats for each trade. This way they could spot a particular trade from a distance. This worked out fine, except once in a while when we traded hats with another department.

We were shoveling snow off the main deck of a navy ship one morning when we saw somebody watching us with binoculars. We all were in the same trade and wore tan hard hats. A short time later, we went to coffee and switched hard hats with welders working below decks. The welders' hats were dark brown. After coffee, we went back up to the main deck and picked up our own shovels and just hung around talking and leaning on our shovels. We did this until we spotted the man in the office building with the binoculars. We then went below and put our tan hard hats back on and started shoveling snow again. Within ten minutes, a welding boss showed up and started looking around. He finally asked us where the welders were working. We told him there were no welders working in the area. He said he got a call from some big shot in an office building reporting there was a crew of welders on the main deck hanging around. He said the welders all had shovels but were not using them. He told the welding boss he had observed these men for 45 minutes and they had not done any work in all that time. After he left, our boss showed up and we told him about the whole incident. We all had a good laugh at the expense of the welding department.

After a short layoff at the yard, I got a recall notice to report to work. I was assigned to the third shift in the steel mill. I disliked the steel mill and the third shift. After being stuck on the third shift for a couple of months, I went and spoke to my superintendent. I asked if I could work on the second shift outside in the yard. He told me the next day to report to a boss by the name of Bill Brock on the second shift at No. 2 platen. The following Monday I came in a little early and met a bunch of second shift workers milling around 2 platen. I asked them about this boss by the name of Bill Brock. Everyone I asked said the same thing. One of the worst bosses in the yard. Now I had done it. Looks like I was going from the frying pan into the fire. One guy told me there was a second shift over on 6 plat and Jim Lobb was the boss. I knew this boss and he was a decent person to work for. I walked over to 6 plat and found Jim Lobb. I told him I had just got off the third shift and was told to report to him on 6 plat on the second shift. Jim said that he had not been told anything about it. He assigned me a job and said he would check out my transfer at the office. I worked for him for over a year and he never said a word about it. Every time I saw him approach me during the first month I worked for him, I figured he was going to say, "You are supposed to be working for Bill Brock on 2 plat." After working for him on 6 plat for about six months, I told him how I picked him for a boss and we both had a good laugh over it. He told me that years before, when he was an hourly paid worker, he had pulled the same switch twice and got away with it. The place was so big and at times so badly organized you could get away with a lot.

Some of the riggers we worked with were excellent, others were practically useless, and some were downright dangerous. One we worked with was called "Dino". He spoke poor English and was scared of his job even though he worked there many years. The rigger's job in our area consisted mainly of attaching the crane to pieces of steel with various devices and then signaling the crane operator by hand signals to pick up the material and place it where the rigger told him to. The cranes were on railroad tracks and could cover a wide area. Dino was so scared of the cranes he would attach the crane to the piece, give the signal to the crane operator and then run, all the while yelling, "Watch out, watch out" in his broken English. The material being moved would weigh anywhere from 100 pounds to 100 tons. To see a rigger run from the crane and at the same time yell "watch out, watch out" didn't instill much confidence in the men working in the area, especially when the crane swung the material over their heads.

Dino was from the Caribbean and suffered terribly in the winter time from the cold. He was a little overweight and in the winter time, he wore so much clothing he looked like a penguin and waddled when he walked. We used to say if he fell over he would never get up without help. He used to wear a set of thermal underwear, two pairs of pants, a flannel shirt, three sweaters, a light jacket and an overcoat over everything. Also a scarf. On bitter cold days, he also wore a ski mask with only his eyes showing. You could never find him on cold nights when you wanted the crane to lift something. Sometimes a person would spend one half hour looking for Dino, checking all the warming shacks and the rest rooms. When he was finally found, it would take him another 15 minutes to dress and get on the job. By this time, I used to almost lose interest in the job I was doing.

We worked with another rigger who was stone deaf in one ear and had a partial hearing loss in the other. When we worked with him, we had to yell to get him to understand us.

Many amusing things happened working with the riggers and cranes. One day, Terry the rigger was hooking up the crane to a piece of material. He had one hand on the material and with the other he was about to give the signal to the crane operator when the material started moving. His glove got caught on the material and he was picked right off the ground. All the while he was yelling at the crane and trying to get the glove off. When he was about 10 feet off the deck, the crane operator realized what was going on and lowered him to the deck. This crane operator had a bad habit of anticipating the rigger's signals before they were actually given. This is what had happened in this case. He started lifting the material before he was signaled to. Terry looked like a fish on a line, flipping and flopping around and yelling at the crane operator. We all laughed at Terry which made him even madder.

Larry was another rigger who was a colorful character. He was a very hard worker. His two biggest faults were being stubborn as a mule and shooting off his mouth. His favorite name for everybody was "Hey a——h——". He would work at an excellent pace as long as he could do everything his way. A new rigging boss took over our area and Larry had never met him. We were working away one night when Larry yelled, "Hey a—h—". I looked to see who was there and it was the new rigging boss. He did not bat an eyelid at this greeting. He very calmly said to Larry, "Have you seen Agga". Larry replied, "Agga who?". To this, the rigging boss replied, "Agga f—yourself". It was the only time I ever saw Larry at a loss for words. This was the start of a very bad relationship. Larry eventually transferred out of our area.

We were busy one day when a loud crashing sound came from an adjacent area. The first thing I looked at was all the cranes in our area. The boom on one close by was shaking. I ran over and a bunch of men were standing there all looking stunned. Two cranes were moving a 95 ton unit and the crane wire snapped on one crane. The unit had dropped to the ground a distance of about 20 feet. A rigger was missing and everybody who was there said he had been under the unit. Suddenly he stepped out from behind the unit. I have never seen a man so pale. His face was drained of all color. It was especially noticeable on him as he had been in the Navy 20 years and normally had a ruddy red weather-beaten face. He had to sit for awhile because he was so shaken.

The next day the unit was repaired and the unit was picked up and moved. The blacktop where the unit had fallen was six inches thick. The corner of the unit had punched a hole completely through all six inches. One side of the unit was badly bent. After inspection, the unit was found to be damaged worse than originally had been thought. Most of one side and some of the structural members on the bottom were found to be damaged and were replaced. The crane wire that had snapped was tested a week before for 85 tons and we all wondered why it broke. It only had a load on it of about 45 to 50 tons. Another serious accident where, luckily, nobody was hurt.

Ace was a welder that worked in our area quite often. He was an older man who was not overly ambitious. He also liked to talk. The best spot for him was usually out of sight by himself with no one to talk to. Ace's boss always had a hard time getting a days work out of him so the boss would frequently put him in an area out of sight. One afternoon, we were working aboard ship back in the stern directly over the rudder. Access into this area was difficult. The stern was reinforced with many bulkheads horizontal and vertical. The bulkheads were about two feet apart and four and one-half feet tall and had 18 inch diameter access holes. To get back into the stern, it was necessary to climb through about 15 of these access holes. Right back into the stern of the ship was a small compartment that was only partially welded. Ace's boss figured there was about 40 hours work there and it would be a good spot for Ace to work. So he climbed back to the job with Ace and showed him the job and congratulated himself on finding a good spot to hide Ace for a week.

This boss was not the ambitious type himself. At least once every day he would position himself by the first access hole and yell, "Hey, Ace." Ace would appear back at the 15th access hole. The boss would always yell, "How's it going?" Ace would hold up his right hand and with thumb and forefinger joined form a circle, commonly known as the signal for A-OK or good. This went on all week—the boss yelling to ask Ace how he was doing and Ace holding up his hand giving the A-OK signal.

By the end of the week, the boss finally decided to crawl into the compartment to check on Ace's progress. He crawled in and there was Ace sitting in the corner reading. He figured Ace must have completed the job. When he looked around, he saw that Ace had only done about eight hours work the entire week. He was furious to say the least. Ace, as usual, was nonchalant. The boss yelled at him, "Every day when I asked you 'How's it going?' you always indicated 'fine'." Ace said I always held up my hand and made a circle with my thumb and forefinger." The boss said, "Where I come from that means 'fine'." Ace said, "Where I come from that means zero." A shouting match followed with the final result that Ace came out on top as usual. The boss could not turn him in to the office. He had been just as guilty as Ace by never climbing in every day and inspecting the progress of the job. Ace knew this and as usual had the last laugh.

A large number of the men in the yard commuted a great distance to work. Public transportation to the yard was excellent; however, many people lived many miles beyond the bus lines. Some of the workers commuted 60–70 miles to work and usually belonged to car pools. A few brought their own cars and drove the long distance by themselves. This was expensive and wore out a car very fast. A few workers that lived a long distance away bought 8–10 passenger vans. These van owners ran a regular bus service from the outlying areas. They made enough money to pay for their vans and $50 to $100 a week extra. When there was overtime, which was often, everybody was expected to work overtime. People who were in a car pool or were the drivers of car pools always had a good excuse for not working overtime. If they felt like taking a day off, they could always say their driver never showed up to take them to work.

One man on our crew took a lot of time off. He always used the same excuse: "My driver didn't show up." This went on for many months before the boss found out he was not in a car pool and only lived about a mile and a half from the yard. Another worker never came to work whenever it snowed. He told the boss that the city didn't plow his street because it was a private street. This went on all winter before the boss found out he lived right across the street from the yard. He walked to work and never even used his car.

The shipyard had many artists besides bull artists. A lot of trades used chalk or crayons for marking purposes. Many men would while away time waiting for stock or another trade to finish their job by drawing pictures or writing essays or sayings on walls. The whole shipyard was one big blackboard. Some of the drawings were excellent. The ship was the best blackboard of all with thousands of square feet to write or draw on. One big easel!! I had a job one night down in an enormous tank on an oil tanker. Somebody must have spent hours with yellow chalk drawing a huge picture of a three masted ship on a bulkhead. The following night, they had added all the rope and fittings, figures on the ships, even an ocean with waves for the ship to float in. It was a shame that the painters would eventually paint over it.

There was all the usual graffiti on the toilet walls. Most of it not very original or unusual. Some of it was a repeat of sayings I had seen since I was a kid. Once in a while I would see something original and clever. One of my favorites read "With all this prose and wit you would think the ghost of Shakespeare had come to shit." Some of it was very crude and offensive to anyone with any sense of decency.

The yard would periodically paint over the toilet walls. They would no sooner paint them and the artists would write and draw over them again in a matter of weeks. The company at one time considered putting up pads of paper in every stall to give the doodlers something to write on. I don't think it would have worked. They would much rather have a big surface to write on where their handiwork could be seen by all.

There were some lazy people working at the yard. Altogether, a great bunch of guys but also many thieves and other assorted riff-raff. Some of the workers would punch in their time cards, get their work assignment from the boss, and then leave at lunch time. Then, they would get another worker to punch out their time card at quitting time. The place was so big with so many people working there the bosses could not check all the workers to see if they were on the job. Two co-workers had been doing this for months before the boss finally caught up to them. One would leave early one day and the other one the next day.

One day, the boss took a head count at quitting time. He had 23 men working for him but there were only 22 at quitting time. The following day, he asked the guilty party where he was at quitting time and the man had no answer. He was docked for four hours pay. Within a week they were skipping out early again. They and many more people continued doing this all the years I was there. If a boss got wise to this scheme, men would leave at lunch and then come back in with the next shift's workers shortly before their own quitting time. Some would even jump the fence and come back six to seven hours later and make an appearance with the boss and then punch out their time cards and go home. Other workers would congregate in isolated areas of the yard and read, play cards, sleep, or just loaf. The yard did their best to curb these practices.

For years, we had fires in open barrels for warmth. A few years back, in an effort to help stop air pollution the State said no more open fires. Management loved this because it was felt the men spent too much time breaking up wood and huddling around fires. One hated boss in particular, "Mother", was fond of say-ing, "A busy worker was a warm worker" as he went back into his heated office and we all froze in the ten degree temperatures with the howling winds and snow. If there is a colder place than a shipyard in the northern climes in the winter, I would not like to visit it.

We were warned that anyone caught making a fire would be disciplined, but we still persisted in making our fires. One cold wintry night, we had a nice warm fire going in a thirty gallon rubbish barrel. "Mother" came by and spotted it. As usual, he kicked it over. Within an hour we had another going which he kicked over and proceeded into his heated office. We decided to fix him. We stood the barrel up and welded it to the deck. Sure enough, he spotted it going again and gave it a fierce kick. He almost broke his ankle. We all had a good laugh over that one.

We had to find a way to keep warm, so we got together with the carpenters and built a fine plywood shack. The welders used a metal hose hooked up to a fan which exhausted welding smoke and gases out of tight areas. After much plan-ning and discussion, we built a wood burning stove with a three inch hole on the back. This was hooked up to one of the welding hoses. This was connected to a welders fan a hundred feet away and camouflaged. The smoke coming out of the fan was assumed to be welding smoke. By the time "Mother" discovered our stove, the cold was over for the year.

The company provided many parking lots. Most of these were well lit. Even with the lighting and frequent checks by the security guards, there was much thievery. Sometimes it would be the contents of cars. Other times, it would be parts or the whole car. One night, I got out of work, got into my car, and started it. I drove away. After about one half mile, the car started slowing down. The engine was running fine but the car kept going slower and slower. I coasted over to the side of the road and opened the hood. When the hood was opened, I was enveloped in a cloud of steam. I thought the radiator had overheated. When the steam cleared, something looked wrong. Then I realized what it was. Somebody had stolen my radiator. My automatic transmission cooling lines had been hooked up to the radiator. When the radiator was stolen, the lines had been cut. All my transmission fluid had drained out and this was why the car had slowed down.

A young worker told me about a car parts ring that operated in the area. He said if I ever needed any part for my car, to let him know. He said that within a week or two, he could secure a part I needed. I asked him how this was done. He said that with all the parking lots scattered around the yard, his friends could find a car with the parts I needed. He said that in the parking lots there was almost every make and model year of any car sold in the last ten years. I told him about what had happened to my radiator and he got a big laugh out of it. I didn't think it was very funny.

Once in a while, somebody would try to start their car and find their battery was missing. If your battery was stolen, it was a no-no to park in the same lot the next night with your new battery. The thieves knew you had a <u>new</u> battery.

After work one night, a friend of mine went to the parking lot and his car was gone. He called the local police to report his car stolen. It was not until quite a while later that we found out what actually happened. It was a new car and he had not been making his time payments. The finance company knew where he worked and they had sent somebody down and repossessed the car. A coworker of mine worked a double shift one night. When he got out to the parking lot, his car was up on four milk cases. Somebody had stolen all four wheels, tires and all. After this incident, he started parking in a private lot. The private lots were on someone's property usually with their house nearby. The company lots were free; the private lots charged a fee, but were much more secure.

Some of the bosses in the yard were hated. We had a superintendent who was hated by everybody because he was constantly harassing people. Many times he had been threatened verbally by workers. Over a period of time, many different incidents happened to him. He went into a restroom after a man who he thought was spending too much time in there. An agreement broke out and the worker punched the super in the face. Another time, he was driving around the yard in a company pickup truck and a steel wedge came through his windshield. Eventually, he got the word and mellowed somewhat.

We had one young boss who was going to set the world on fire. He never had enough to do and used to spend the whole shift snooping around. One night, he went out to the parking lot and found all the windows broken in his car. Another night he went out and found all his tires had been slashed.

One of the worst incidents happened to a third shift super. He was aboard ship one night when somebody emptied a five gallon paint bucket on him from about 50 feet over his head. As it fell, it fanned out so he did not feel the full weight of the paint. Still, he was covered from head to toe. He was rushed to First Aid and had to have a shower and a good scrubdown from head to foot. The First Aid man said that it was lucky for him it was water-soluble latex paint. If it had been oil paint or epoxy paint, he might have had serious eye damage.

During the years I worked there, a few bosses were assaulted by the workers and I knew of one boss who resigned rather than take all the abuse from the people on his crew. His crew at the time consisted of many of the hard core people that the government had forced the yard into hiring. As the work force of the yard fluctuated with the amount of work, so did the bosses. When the work force was large, the company would promote people into management. Some people were promoted to a position called working leader or straw boss. They remained in the union but were usually put in charge of four to twelve men. When there was a reduction in force layoff, these working leaders were put back working with the tools.

One man I knew, by the name of Joe, had a working leader's position for about a year. After a reduction in force layoff, he went back to the tools. A short time later the yard acquired more work and more people were hired. Joe got his working leaders job back. He had the job back for about a year and there was another reduction in force layoff. Again, Joe went back to the tools. At the time, his super told him when work picked up he would get the working leaders job back as he had before. A few months later, work picked up and Joe was told he was going to get his working leaders job back. After a few weeks, a minority worker got the job instead. Joe went to the super and asked why the job had been given to someone else. The super said it was out of his hands. Joe questioned him and the super said the front office had told him a minority had to be put on the working leader's job. Joe argued that he had been told the job was his and also that he was much better qualified by experience and proven ability. Joe got an appointment with the front office and they told him that the reason for putting someone else on the job was that the company wanted to try someone else on the job. They told him that he had done an excellent job in the past and it was no reflection on his ability in awarding the job to another man. On further questioning, they would not admit that the minority issue had entered into their selection in any way. Joe became very disillusioned with the company after this incident.

The super in our department believed that everyone should have his coffee break on the job but the workers liked to have their coffee break together. When the weather was cold they would all congregate in the office or a warming shack at coffee time. If the super caught them in the office or a warming shack he would order them out and threaten to discipline them.

One cold day at coffee time my partner and I tried to get into a warming shack. The shack was full so we went over to the office. As we approached the office I could see that it was full. I opened the door and told the men having coffee that the super was walking towards the office. I almost got run over by the people running out of the office. Right after they left, my partner and I went in, sat down, and had our coffee. We were only in the office five minutes when one of the men who had been in the office stuck his head in the door and said, "Where is the super?" I said, "What super?" He screamed, "You said the super is coming." I laughed and he left slamming the door behind him. Within five minutes, all the men we had evicted were back in the office having coffee. The difference was now we had the chairs and they were standing. We laughed over that one for a while.

A man that I worked with had a slight speech impediment. One day, while we were working together, his stuttering became progressively worse during the course of the day. I did not want to say anything to hurt his feelings but towards the end of the day he was stuttering so badly I could hardly understand him. Curiosity finally got the better of me and I asked him why he was stuttering so badly. He said very clearly without stuttering, "How does it sound?" I said, "I could hardly understand you a minute ago." He said, "Tomorrow I have to go to the Veteran's Administration". Periodically, he had to go and see a speech doctor at the VA. He claimed his speech impediment was service connected and he got a 40% disability for the impediment. If he talked normally, he was afraid they would cut his disability to 25% or less. So, he had been practicing his stuttering al day to impress the VA doctor.

The next day, he went to the VA. The following day he came into work. I asked him how he had made out at the VA. He laughed and said very clearly, "I guess I must have really sounded rough because they are going to raise my disability to 50%." As long as I worked with him, he hardly stuttered, but periodically, the day before he was going into the VA, he would practice till he had it down pat. As long as I knew him, he got his check every month for the 50%. Seems like everyone who worked there had one angle or another to make a little extra money.

Periodically, the company tried to enforce the rule of wearing safety glasses. This was ignored by some workers and some bosses. For a period of about two weeks they would insist that everyone wore glasses. If you didn't, you would get a chit. Hardhats were one thing; glasses another. Nobody wanted to wear them. After about two weeks, less and less people would be wearing their glasses. Within a matter of months, somebody would have an eye injury. The order would come to wear glasses and for another two weeks, everybody would comply. Wearing glasses was awkward. When a person sweats, the glasses would slide down his nose. When it was damp, they would fog up. You couldn't keep them clean. After dark in poorly lit areas, they were hazardous as they impaired your vision. A shipyard is a dangerous place during the day, but after dark, it took on a whole new dimension. Shadows everywhere, rubbish, piles of jagged steel, holes, etc. You really had to be on the ball and glasses were definitely a hazard. I used to get in some bad arguments with the boss about wearing them after dark. We finally compromised and I agreed to wear them only in well lit areas.

We always had a bunch of comedians at the yard and many of them loved to play practical jokes on their co-workers. One night, a burner took a piece of flat stock about 24 inches long and welded a cross piece to this near the top about eighteen inches wide. This roughly resembled a cross. Across this, he put a coat and a hard hat with a welder's shield under the hard hat. This was taken on a ladder to the top of a bulkhead, about thirty feet above the ground and draped over the top of the bulkhead with one arm hanging down with glove attached. Into the glove he placed a welder's stinger. The burner then took the ladder down and hid it. From ground level, it looked like a welder hanging over the top of the bulkhead, welding. Then he called the yard safety engineer and said his name was Jim Hennigan. The safety engineer asked what his problem was and he told him he was a welder working on a unit with unsafe working conditions. The safety engineer wrote down the area of the yard he was working in, the unit he was working on, and his boss's name. The safety engineer walked down to the area and found the boss and asked him where Jim Hennigan was working and he replied that he did not have anybody by that name working for him and furthermore, he did not have any welders working on that unit. The safety engineer walked over to the unit and saw the welder hanging over the top of the unit and yelled up to him by name. Jim did not answer so he yelled up to him again. No answer. We were all working in the area and most of us were wise as to what was going on. The safety engineer then asked the welding boss if there were any more welding crews working in the area. He said no and they both tried to figure out who the man was hanging over the top of the unit. The engineer tried to figure out how the welder had got up on the unit without a ladder. The two of them asked a couple of workers in the immediate area who the welder was on the unit and how long he had been up there. After about ten more minutes of yelling at Jim on the unit with no response, they got the carpenters to put up a ladder. Up they climbed onto the unit, flashlight in hand. By this time, most of the workers in the area knew what was going on and we were just about killing ourselves laughing. A short time later, the welding boss and safety engineer climbed down from the unit, both upset that they had been had. The word was spread around later on that night that if anybody was caught goofing off, he would receive a chit.

Some of the union workers delighted in pulling off schemes to make an individual boss or the company look foolish. The safety engineer on our shift was rather gullible and the butt of many practical jokes. He had been appointed to the job by the head of the safety department. The rumor was that the head of the department and the safety engineer had both been in the Marines Corps together. When this safety engineer had worked with the tools, he had many accidents. Some people even went so far as to say he was accident prone. These same people used to say the main reason he was appointed to the job was his years of experience in the yard. Not so much his working experience but his accident experiences. You name the accident, he had experience in it. Broken bones, burns, contusions, abrasions, lacerations, stitches, etc. It was comforting knowing we had a First Aid man with all this experience!

We used to have a once a week safety discussion. This would usually be after lunch. The safety department would give the foreman a few paragraphs to read to his crew. Every week it would involve a different topic. One week it would be dressing for the cold weather, another week it would be on the hazards of working off ladders and stagings, another week, on the hazards of working with or near burning torches. The company made a good effort to preach and practice safety.

At times, though, when they had a deadline to make, it seemed like safety would go out the window. One job in particular was way behind schedule. Everybody was working overtime under very poor working conditions. Staging was broken or nonexistent. Lights were broken or missing. Ventilation was inadequate and there was a lot of rubbish and jagged steel lying about. Everybody was complaining about it and somebody asked the boss to have the area cleaned up and the safety hazards corrected. He said he would look into this, but after two days, nothing was done. The boss was then asked to call the safety man to come to the job. He said he would, but the safety man never came.

On the fourth day, the safety man happened to be walking by the area. Somebody spotted him and asked him to come up onto the job and have a look around. He said he would, but he was in a hurry to go to the site of an accident. He promised to come back later on in the shift.

He never showed up. The next day, I ran into him in the yard and asked him if he was going to come on the job and have some of the hazards corrected. He said he had orders not to go on that particular job. So much for safety. He had the authority to shut down a job and stop the men from working on it. This, he sometimes did much to the distress of the bosses on the job, but if a job was running behind schedule, it was sometimes a different story and he would be ordered to stay away from that particular job. He was such a thorn in the side of some of the big bosses that they managed to have him transferred off our shift. For a period of months, we had no safety man on our shift that we could call. A few months later, after we had a few serious accidents and after many requests, we managed to get our safety man back.

On the second shift, if a person was sick or injured, the firemen would have to transport him to the nearest hospital. One night, I was working with the cranes and jammed my finger between two pieces of steel. After taking off my glove and examining my finger, I saw that I had a very deep laceration with possible tendon damage. I went up to First Aid and the corpsman said I would have to go to the hospital for stitches. At the time, there was a man on one of the First Aid station beds who appeared to be having trouble breathing. The corpsman said that he was trying to get the yard firemen to transport this man to the hospital in the company ambulance. He tried to reach them at the fire station, but as it turned out later, they were fighting a fire in the yard. Meanwhile, the man on the bed was having a hard time breathing and was getting progressively worse so the corpsman decided he would drive the ambulance himself. He went outside to start the ambulance. After a short time, he came back in and said it would not start. He asked me to see if I could start it. I went out and turned the key in the ignition, but nothing happened. We thought it must have had a dead battery.

When he called the fire station again, the firemen had returned. One of them came right over and started the ambulance. A kill switch had been installed under the dashboard. The keys were useless unless this switch was also tripped. The ill man on the bed was carried into the ambulance and the corpsman, the driver, and I got in. The corpsman administered oxygen to the man on the stretcher as we drove to the hospital. It was the wildest ride I ever had. The siren wailed constantly and we ran every red light all the way. The ill man who I thought was having a heart attack recovered and I got three stitches. I found out later that the man was a welder and he was suffering from smoke inhalation from welding fumes. I don't know what would have happened if the man had a heart attack.

I came back to the yard about 9:30 PM, went to First Aid, got my medical clearance and reported back to work. I had not had any supper and it had been about seven hours since I had a meal. Was I starved! My lunchbox was on the job site and I knew I had pastry, a sandwich, and soup. When I opened my lunchbox, everything was gone but the soup. I was furious. Along came a co-worker, Bill the burner, and I asked him about my lunch. He said he had seen me leave in the ambulance right before supper and didn't think I would be back that night. He said he didn't think I would need any lunch so he ate it himself. He very nonchalantly added that the pastry was good, but I should tell my wife to add more mayonnaise to the tuna as it was too dry. With this, I became even madder than before. He was wearing a pair of burners' goggles attached to his hard hat by a rubber band. I reached out and grabbed the goggles with the intention of stretching them out and letting them go to bounce off his forehead. He grabbed my fingers with his hand and put pressure on my recent stitches. He was too far away to strike so I let go with my size 13 boot and caught him "where the sun don't shine" and lifted him about a foot off the deck. He let go and so did I. After this, I sat down and had my soup.

I was quite surprised that he had eaten my lunch, but after thinking about and knowing the person involved, I really was not surprised. I had known him most of my life and he was a likable person, with one bad fault. He had more nerve than anybody I have ever met. He smoked pot quite heavily and sold some once in a while to his co-workers. One day, a co-worker wanted to buy an ounce of pot from him. The price was agreed on and they agreed to make the sale the following day. The next day the man said he wanted to have a look at the goods before he bought them. Bill told him where the pot was stashed and the man said he would have a look. A short time later, Bill checked out his stash and found that the pot was missing. He asked the buyer for the money and the buyer said he had changed his mind and did not want the pot.

Later, Bill was working with me and told me what happened. I asked him how he was going to get his money and he said that he was not concerned about his money but he had already made a phone call to a "friend" who was going to fix the man's van out in the parking lot. An hour later, the pot turned up where it had been stashed. I asked Bill what he was going to do about the man's van seeing that he had got his pot back. He said nothing. I said, "You mean you aren't going to call your 'friend' and tell him to lay off the man's van?" He said, "No, and it would serve the man right for taking his pot." I said, "You got your pot back," and he said, "That's the breaks." That night when the buyer went out to the parking lot, his van had a smashed windshield and four slashed tires.

On Friday nights after work we used to go to a local bar for a few drinks after work. This one night, Bill came along and said that his wife was going to pick him up one hour after work at the bar. About five of us were sitting at a table talking when a young lady came along and said to Bill that she would like to talk to him alone. They went over to another table and had a heated discussion, parts of which we could overhear. He came back to our table quite agitated and said that she had said he was spreading lies about her. Seems that they had gone out together and she claimed he had said she was easy. Somebody asked him what he had said back to her and he said he told her to get laid. He no sooner told us this and his wife came into the bar and joined us at the table. The other girl saw her and came over and the three of them started arguing. We got up and left. Bill ended up walking home.

About this time, one quart stainless steel Thermos bottles were getting popular in the yard. There were lots of coffee machines throughout the yard but a lot of men preferred to bring their own coffee because half the time, the machines would take your money and deliver no coffee or coffee without milk or sugar. The yard issued many tools to the workers and a lot of thieving of company property went on. There was an unwritten law in the yard that it was all right to take company tools but never steal a man's personal tools. This was like taking food out of his children's mouths. These stainless steel Thermos bottles were unbreakable and highly prized. A new one cost about $25.00. Many men on my crew bought them and everybody agreed they were great and would last a lifetime. Bill, one day, announced he intended to acquire a Thermos. Within a few days, he had the Thermos and I asked him how much he paid for it. He said nothing. He claimed that he found it on board ship. His story was that someone on the earlier shift had gone home at quitting time and left it on the dock. I found out later that the owner had gone to the men's room and when he came back, the Thermos was gone. They all looked the same so he had no way of proving it was his. It got so you didn't trust this man working with you if you had any personal tools lying about. I questioned him about this one day and he said he would never take anything that belonged to a friend. As far as I knew, he never did.

LNGs and the Goliath Crane

The yard secured a contract for 10 huge 936 foot liquefied natural gas tankers (LNG). There were two elements to the construction of these mammoth ships. One was building the huge aluminum spheres to carry the gas on the ships, and the other was building a large crane to pick up the spheres and place them aboard ship. The LNGs would be built here at this yard. Twelve years before, we had built a 1,000 foot tanker of over 100,000 tons, the *Manhattan*. When the keel for this mammoth tanker had been laid in the late 1950's it was, up until that time, the heaviest ship built anywhere in the world.

A contract was awarded to a company in South Carolina to build the 120 foot aluminum spheres to carry the gas. Another contract was let to build a 1200 ton crane. It would measure over 350 feet high and span an area of about 400 feet. With its lifting capacity of 1200 tons, it would lift more tonnage than any other crane of its type in the world.

Work went ahead on the LNGs and three ships were launched and waited for the aluminum spheres. The reason the spheres took so long to build was that nobody had ever built aluminum spheres this big before (120 feet) or welded aluminum this thick (about three inches). The technology had to be developed on site as the spheres were being built. Construction and welding of the spheres was like sailing into unknown and uncharted waters.

We had been hearing rumors that the company that was making the spheres was having trouble completing the first sphere. The company building them did not have the know how for the job. Even though the yard sent many engineers to the job site to assist this company, after many months, there was no significant progress. Finally, the yard bought out the company and spent many millions of dollars constructing a new facility. One of the new buildings was the largest building in the state of South Carolina.

Meanwhile work went ahead in the fabricating and construction of the crane in Quincy. The largest rigging company in New England was awarded a contract to erect the crane. Four enormous legs were built. Two legs were erected on each side and the center span was fitted together on the ground. The legs were braced with guy wires. The center span was welded together and wires were connected from the ends of the center span to the tops of the legs. The riggers started lifting the span and when it was about 50 feet off the ground, all progress stopped. The riggers walked off the job saying it was unsafe.

A large weld had cracked on the center span. The yard rushed fitters and welders to repair the damage. The rigging company said that the method of hoisting the center span was unsafe and refused to continue the job. The yard said it was safe. Both companies said they were right. Finally the yard itself took over the job and the span was successfully raised.

A whole series of concrete blocks had been constructed on the ground. These were to serve as test weights for the crane. All together, these test weights weighed 1600 tons. Small weights were used initially for test lifts. Heavier and heavier weights were lifted until 1600 tons were suspended from the crane. These weights were suspended from three different hooks on the crane. Each hook was rated for 400 tons. They now were successfully holding 400 tons total more than they had been rated for. This extra tonnage was a safety factor that all rigging gear was subjected to. A series of wires leading down from the hooks held the weights. Suddenly, all the test weights dropped a few feet and stopped abruptly! A piece of gear connected to the wires had slipped out of place. Sixteen hundred tons had dropped and suddenly stopped. This was not part of the test. The crane was inspected and no damage resulted from this sudden fall. It was agreed by everybody that a better test could never have been devised. Not only had the crane lifted 1600 tons and held it stationery, but it had held under the additional load of the weights dropping and stopping short.

After the center span of the crane had been raised into place, many yard workers were pressed into service finishing off all the related jobs on the crane. Most of this work was done on the top of the center span. Many workers were afraid of height and wanted no part of this job. Other workers wanted to work on it. There was plenty of overtime. On this job, the company was paying the workers about double their normal rate of pay in the yard.

When the crane went into service, it was completely computerized. The operator had total control over it and it ran very smoothly. It could move back and forth up and down and sideways 1/8 inch at a time. It even had a built in safety switch that killed the power if the wind blew over 40 MPH. It is now a landmark in the area and can be seen for many miles in any direction.

It was summertime and the crane was a great place to work. The view was spectacular and on clear days; it seemed to be endless. Since many of the jobs required a particular trade to stand by for hours at a time, soon the yardbirds began designing small parachutes to launch from this great height. Contests were held to see which parachute would stay aloft the longest. On windy days, other contests were held to see which parachute would cover the greatest distance before touchdown. After a while, all the spare rags disappeared for the manufacture of parachutes. One yardbird even tore up his tee shirt for parachute material.

Styrofoam coffee cups proved to be almost as good floaters as parachutes. One windy day, one cup won the distance contest. It floated on the wind about 2/3 of a mile before touch down.

One of the few bad things about working on the top of the crane was getting there. Inside of one of the huge legs was a series of stairways. It took about 15 breathless minutes to climb to the top. The only other way was to climb in a safety bucket and be hoisted up by a large service crane that had been placed alongside the crane. The ride up in the bucket was much quicker and easier but a little on the scary side. Sometimes the service crane that was used to hoist us to the top would be out of commission. When this happened, we had to climb to the top inside the leg on a stairway. It took some of the overweight, older workers a long time to reach the top. One day, I decided to climb all the way to the top nonstop. I made it without a break. The welding boss on the job told me he didn't think any one else had done this nonstop. Once was enough. Boy, was I out of breath when I got to the top!

One rigger working on top with us did stupid, scary things. It was about 350 feet from the top of the box girder to the ground. A safety rail was installed completely around the girder to keep people safe. This idiot used to like to walk on the outside of the rail tempting fate. He even did it on windy nights. From the edge of the girder to the safety rail was about thirty inches and this idiot used to prance around in this area. It was scary! He was a young kid and us guys who had been around a while and witnessed a few fatal accidents did not like this. After a few complaints to the rigging foreman, he was reassigned to work on the ground, much to our relief.

One afternoon I snuck a camera into the yard and brought it up to the top of the crane. I couldn't have picked a better day. The visibility was superb. As the saying goes, "You could see forever". Mount Graylock, the highest mountain in Massachusetts, was visible to the west about 135 miles away. I took many pictures including about a dozen in a circular arc. When arranged on a table in a circle, the complete south and north shores of Massachusetts was visible, including all the islands.

More months dragged by and finally the rumor circulated that the first sphere had been completed. A short time later, the sphere was walked out of its huge assembly building in South Carolina. It was lowered into its tailor made cradle aboard the specially designed barge *Hercules* for its one thousand mile trip up the coast to Quincy. The barge built to carry these 120 foot spheres was massively built with hundreds of twelve inch by twelve inch I-beams installed below the deck to back up the cradle carrying the 900 ton aluminum spheres. This barge was without a doubt one of the strongest barges ever built. It was quite a sight seeing this huge 120 foot bright yellow "beach ball" coming up the Atlantic coast. I often wondered what would happen if one broke loose in a storm and drifted into a beach. It would be the world's biggest bright yellow beach ball.

A short time after the arrival of the first sphere, the company opened up the yard for a celebration. Relatives and friends were invited and food and refreshments were served. As part of the celebration, the first sphere was lifted off the barge and placed onboard the LNG. This was indeed a very happy day for the yard and all the workers. The very future of this yard depended on the ability of the company to build these spheres. Each ship required five of these spheres and it soon became a regular and common occurrence for one of these spheres to arrive by barge. Within a short time, the company was building spheres faster than the yard could build the ships to hold them. These ships went into service and are now widely recognized as the best LNGs in the world.

One day, as we were looking at the side of one of the LNG ships, somebody commented that it was an enormous mass of steel exposed to the wind. He made a quick calculation as to the total surface. We were surprised at the area, over one acre of steel. A few weeks later, we saw what the wind could do pressing on this huge mass of steel. A LNG was eased out of its berth by six tugboats. As it entered the river, the wind started pushing on the side of the ship. The six tugs strained to turn the ship into the wind. It soon became apparent that they were fighting a losing battle with the wind. The amazing part to me was the wind was only blowing about 20 miles an hour. The river was narrow at this point and the huge ship slowly started moving sideways down the river. The tugs were all pushing for all their worth. They were able to slow the ship but could not turn her.

A few hundred yards down the river, the river made a right angle turn. At this turn in the river, there was an oil tank farm and a dock where the tankers tied up to unload at the tank farm. The LNG was pushed slowly down river towards this dock. The decision was made to guide her alongside this dock and hold her there till the wind died down. The tugs eased her into the dock. Two inch steel cables 2000 or more feet long were run out from the ship and carried back to the shipyard piers by the tugs. The dock that the ship was secured to was designed for 500 foot long oil tankers. It was no match for this 935 foot long ship that was being pushed by the wind. The dock was starting to disintegrate. The cables running back to the yard piers were tightened. Still the wind pushed on the ship and the dock. Suddenly, there was a loud noise not unlike a rifle shot. One of the two inch cables had snapped. A short time later, another cable snapped. A huge four inch nylon hawser was then run out from the ship back to the shipyard pier. This held and the ship and pier were saved. Fortunately, nylon has a lot of stretch and acted like a huge rubber band to keep the ship from crushing the dock. One of the riggers that was aboard ship told me the following day: "I have never seen steel cables snap like that in all my 26 years working here. Without that nylon hawser, the dock would have been crushed and the ship would have been run ashore." After that, the tugboat company said that they would never move another LNG when the wind was over 10 miles per hour.

Things like this did not happen very often. The biggest problem was that these huge ships are made for the open sea. In rivers and small harbors they are helpless as kittens without the tugs. Even with the tugs, they are no match for the wind especially when they are empty and riding high.

Many modern ships have a bow thruster mounted underwater. It is sometimes mounted in the bulbous bow and looks very much like a ceiling fan found in most new homes. This is usually fitted as far forward as possible in a ship. Its purpose is to help the ship maneuver at the dock and in harbors and channels. A circular hole anywhere from 4 feet to 10 feet is cut in the sides of a ship up in the bow. Into this is fitted a huge propeller which can push water on either side of the ship. The propeller is usually powered by a very powerful electric motor and will spin either clockwise or counter-clockwise depending on which way a ship is being maneuvered. These LNGs had the most powerful bow thruster ever installed aboard a ship at that time. I have seen them turning and they push as much water as a powerful tugboat.

One day, the thruster was being tested dockside and a school of pogies was swimming by. As they got near the thruster, they were sucked in and spit out on the other side.

Another interesting feature on many modern ships is the bulbous bow. It had long been thought that the thin knife bow on a destroyer or submarine was the fastest design for a ship. When these ships reached about 20 MPH, huge amounts of power were needed to make them go faster. The faster the ship moved, the bigger a wave it pushed out.

After the Second World War naval architects were asked to design a new modern submarine. This new submarine was to be atomic powered. Scientists and naval architects began studying porpoises, which are some of the fastest creatures in the sea. They discovered the speed these animals produced with their limited horsepower was much faster than man had achieved in ships with more horse-power. Furthermore, these animals speeding through the water put out a very small wave. With this in mind, a radical new design concept was developed. The first atomic sub, the *USS Nautilus,* had a round bow very similar to the head of a porpoise. This was a far cry from the sleek thin bows of World War II subs. The new design proved to be very successful.

All future subs were built in this fashion. Ship models were tested in tanks with this type of bow. The rounded part, or bulbous bow, was added on and only on that part of the bow that was under water. It was found that the models with this type of bow would go 2 to 3 knots faster than a model with a conventional bow with the same horsepower. The models with the bulbous bows made a lot smaller bow wave passing through the water. On further study, it was found that instead of the wave being pushed out and away from the ship in a large vee, it was traveling down the entire length of the ship and wrapping itself around the stern of the ship. This was how a ship fitted with a bulbous bow could be driven through the water two to three knots faster than a ship fitted with a conventional bow.

The only drawback to the bulbous bow on a ship was when it reached a cer-tain speed, whirlpools and eddies would form alongside the ship and slow down the wave traveling towards the stern. The architects found that once the ship reached this speed, about two or three knots faster than a conventional ship, the whirlpools and eddies would start. This did not happen with porpoises. On fur-ther study of these animals, they found that the porpoise's body shape changed as his speed increased. The animal was able to change the contour of his body to suit the water conditions.

The skin of a ship is rigid so that was as far as the architects could go. Still, two to three knots faster is a big advantage for a ship. This was a huge savings on fuel when the life of a ship was taken into consideration. A ship will steam hundreds of thousands of miles in her long lifetime. With a bulbous bow a ship will save thousands of barrels of fuel in her life. Soon small freighters were built with this unique bow. Next it was added on many tankers. Today the bulbous bow is a part of most modern ships.

Sweet and Not So Sweet Young Things

The burner named Bill, besides selling pot, was an industrious scrap metal junkie. Any time he found any lead, brass, copper, etc. on board ship that wasn't nailed down, he would confiscate it. He would melt it down, put it into a second hollow thermos he kept in his locker for this purpose, and then carry it home to sell.

One night he was walking home over the Fore River Bridge and noticed the two very substantial bronze tablets, measuring about two feet by three feet, attached to the foot of the bridge. The tablets, installed when the bridge was built about 1937, described the bridge and also included the architect's, builder's, and governor's names. Bill told me about them and commented that the bronze was probably worth a lot.

About a month later, I was driving home over the bridge and noticed one was missing. Within a month, the other tablet was missing. A person or a city would be wise not to leave anything around with a thief like Bill nearby.

I had a young helper who was a good worker but hated the second shift. He occasionally acted rather oddly and was almost like another person. One night, I gave him an easy job and went on to another job myself. After supper, my boss asked me what job I had assigned to the helper. I told him where the helper was working and he said he was not there. I sensed an urgency in my boss's voice and asked if anything was wrong. He said another foreman reported that my helper was dancing with his sledgehammer near where I had left him. We went down to that deck and he was not there. We searched the whole ship, all the restrooms, and the warming shacks and everywhere we could think of.

About two hours later, we went back to his assigned work area. He was on the job, but not in the way we expected. He was holding his sledge hammer vertically and dancing with it. To make matters even more bizarre, he was singing to it! The guards were called and they escorted him up to First Aid. The corpsman told him to urinate in a jar. He said he didn't have to go. Our shift was over in an hour and he never did use the jar. I never saw the guy again and my boss said he was transferred onto days. Some guys would do anything to get off the second or third shift. I often wondered if this guy was on something or it was his own crazy way to get back on days.

Getting people to work the second and third shift was always difficult. The company would usually have to order people to work these shifts for a specific period of time. There were never enough volunteers and it was a constant battle filling the crews on these shifts. The company didn't like to put women on these shifts after dark because of the problems this presented in dark parts of the yard. The men complained about this loudly. The feeling was that they were given preferential treatment because they were women. The company said that this was not so, but some women were always on the first shift while their male co-workers were transferred onto the second and third shifts.

As more women went to work in the yard more complications arose. A married friend of mine was dating an eighteen year old female welder for quite a while. He was very discreet about it and not many people knew he was dating her. After many months, he stopped seeing her and a few weeks later she quit the company and went back to New Hampshire to live. About six months later, my friend was called up to Personnel one morning. There was his ex-girlfriend with her mother. She had put on about twenty-five pounds, all in her mid section, and her mother wanted to know what my friend Bill was going to do about it. The blessed event was only about two months away. Bill had a new car which he had paid cash for by working very much overtime. He ended up selling the car and giving the proceeds to his ex girl. How he ever explained it to his wife, I don't know.

Some of the girls the company hired were real winners. One beauty was taking on all comers in warming shacks in the yard. Rumors said even some of the bosses were partaking of her favors. She worked aboard ship for a time until the company transferred her to a wide open area of the yard. This slowed down the action for a while, but she was soon up to her old tricks. A short time later, she was involved in a serious car accident. She never came back to work. The rumor was the company flunked her on her physical when she tried to come back to work. Many workers were very unhappy about this sad turn of events.

Some of the girls were nice and some of them married yard birds. I could never figure why a nice girl would want to work there with the horrible working conditions. I finally asked a girl this question and she said in an office, the pay was about $3.50 an hour. Besides the low pay, money had to be spent on a wardrobe that had to be constantly updated. At the yard, they could start at about $5.50 an hour with little money put out for clothes. Within a year, some of them were making $6.75 an hour. One of the girls told me she would rather work with a bunch of guys than a bunch of gossipy women in an office or factory. Most bosses did not like having girls on their crews as it usually caused problems. Most guys did not like having women in the yard because they could not swear and carry on as usual. They didn't change their language or habits. They said if the women wanted to work in the yard, they should be ready for the language and abuse that is common in the yard.

Many girls felt right at home and quickly fit into the routine of the yard. Many others complained about the language and remarks made to them and a few quit because of this atmosphere. Most of them just shrugged it off and realized if they wanted to stay they would have to overlook it. So they did their work and kept their mouths shut. A few wanted the men to help them with anything that weighed over ten pounds. Most of the guys felt that if they were going to be paid the same as the men, they should be expected to do equal work. Once they realized this, things usually worked out. Many women became welders or burners and if they liked the work, they excelled at it. Patience is required of both trades if quality work is to be expected. Many of them picked up the skills required quickly and did excellent work.

One night, a new female welder went to work on a welding gang near us. Her name was Carol. Even with welding leathers and a hard hat, this girl was a knock-out. Later that night, the welding boss remarked to me that this girl was going to be trouble. All the single guys wanted to know her name and did she have a boy-friend.

Every night a welder and two or three riggers and a crane would be assigned to me. My job at that time was erecting steel bulkheads, decks, plates, frames, and other various components that all together would form a unit that would then be worked on by the day shift. When finished, it would be moved over to the ship. These units weighed anywhere from 25 to about 100 tons. We would erect (place) all the pieces in their proper locations on the units and temporarily weld them in place. The braces that held these pieces in place had to be welded <u>very</u> securely. Sometimes, we would have a piece about 30 feet long and 15 feet high weighing about 30 tons held up by three diagonal braces. Needless to say, if the braces gave way, 30 tons would fall on the workers working in that area. We would try to place the pieces within 1/2 inch to one inch of their final location. On the day shift and succeeding shifts it might take one hour to sometimes two days to move these pieces the last 1/2 inch to one inch into place. Heavy metal does not bend and it might take three shifts of men using 50 to 100 or 200 ton hydraulic rams and other equipment to move the piece the last half inch into place. When the pieces were finally in place, welders would weld them up solid.

Modern steel ships have many miles of welds. The temporary braces holding the units together must be welded strongly. Lives depend on this temporary welding.

The welding boss had 15 to 20 men on his crew working in various areas. Many of these areas were isolated and poorly lighted. Each welder would bring along his own extension light, his welding line, and sometimes his own personal exhaust hose to remove the smoke from welding if it was a small, poorly ventilated area.

After the new girl was on the welding crew for about two weeks, the poor boss was having trouble placing her on jobs and still having work progress in that area. Besides being a beautiful, shapely girl, she was also personable, good natured, and would talk to anybody that talked to her. The guys swarmed around her like bees to honey. The welding boss would spend his entire shift checking on the progress his men were making. No matter where he put Carol, she would always have trouble working with all her fans. They would be away from their assigned work areas and they would get in trouble when the boss came around and they were not there.

Some nights I would have three riggers, two cranes, one welder and a fellow shipfitter helping me on big, complicated jobs. Every night the welding foreman would assign a welder to work with us. Most welders liked working with us as they had a lot of standby time waiting for us to erect the steel. About a month after Carol came to work with the welding crew, her boss said to me, almost in desperation, would I take her as our welder one night. I was concerned as she was a fairly new welder and we needed someone who was an excellent welder. He assured me she caught on quick and was a good welder.

So, Carol came to work with us. She turned out to be an excellent welder and worked with us many months. After she worked with us about a week, the welding boss said to me with a sly smile on his face, "I knew Carol would be safe working with you." I didn't know how to take that. From then on, I had fitters and riggers asking me if I needed any more help. Fairly often, we had to weld clips to bulkheads to attach braces about 12 feet off the deck. Carol would climb the ladder and I would climb up after her and lean on her and hold the clip up for her to weld. All of a sudden everybody wanted to climb the ladder and hold the clip. I said, "It's a rough job, but somebody has to do it." Sometimes guys would yell at me, "Watch that stuff." Carol eventually went back onto the day shift and married one of the day shift guys.

One day, a new female burner started work in our area. She was overweight and not attractive at all. Most homely people have at least one attractive feature.

This poor girl had none with one exception: a large chest. She worked with us for many nights.

There was something familiar about this girl and it bugged me for weeks. Where did I know her from? I asked my friend Brownie if he had ever seen her before and he said no. One day Brownie and I were working together and she was working for us. She did not have a long enough burning hose with her to reach our job and started dragging more hose over. Brownie and I stopped working and helped her. She was at least 100 feet away and bent over to grab more hose. Watching her, all of a sudden I realized where I knew her from. I said to Brownie, "Do you read 'BC' in the funnies?" He never answered my question, but said, "The fat broad." The two of us practically fell over laughing. She came running over and wanted to know what was so funny. I could hardly talk and finally said, "You would not understand." She looked puzzled. For the rest of the night, Brownie and I compared her to the "fat broad" (short straight butch haircut, homely, overweight, and a big chest). I asked Brownie when he recognized her and he said when she picked up the hose, she looked just like the "fat broad" beating the snake in the funnies. For the rest of the night every time she dragged her hose, Brownie and I started laughing. She probably thought we were both nuts.

About one year after women came to work in the yard a new female burner come to work with us on the second shift. She was an average looking young lady. She caught on quick and was pleasing to work with and always good natured. She was a nice person. I grew fond of her and was glad when she was assigned to our crew. Some of the burners were grouchy and spent a lot of time goofing off or in the warming shacks. She was always on the job and was cheerful. All of the guys on our crew grew to like her, even the ones who hated seeing women working in the yard. She came to work with us in the summer and worked with us on and off for the better part of a year.

With the advent of warmer weather the following spring, we all started shedding our heavy multiple layers of clothes. We hadn't seen our female burner for about two months because she had been working aboard ship. What a surprise we all got when she came back with our crew after the two months aboard ship. She was noticeably heavier and it wasn't from pizza and hamburgers. As far as we knew nobody on our crew was dating her. As the blessed event grew nearer and nearer, there was much speculation as to who the father was. She would not tell anyone. A few months later, she had a baby boy. One of the riggers saw her about two months later at a local restaurant with the baby and asked her about the baby and herself. She said the baby's name was Alex. The mystery was solved. Our married boss's name was Alex. A few months later, he left the yard and a promising future. The old timers all said girls in the yard were trouble and this proves it. They blamed her for ruining a young guy's future. I commented it takes two to tango.

Anyone who has ever been in the service has heard the term "short arm inspection" and "pecker checker". In the shipyard, many men had trouble changing their language when women came to work in the yard. Some men swore constantly and did not change when the women came to work in the yard. We had a boss like this on our crew. He did not like women in the yard. He said it was no place for a woman to be working and if they did not like the language they didn't have to work there. Once a week, a superintendent comes through our area checking on people. Word always filtered down to our area via the grapevine what day and about what hour of the day the super would be around. After a while, the guys started calling the super "pecker checker". When he came through the area, the guys would warn one another that the "pecker checker" was around. There was one girl on our crew named Betty. One night at the start of our shift the boss gathered the whole crew together including Betty. We were all standing there, Betty included. He started off by saying, "The 'pecker checker' is coming around about 6:00. Everybody better be on the job and working." One man looked at Betty and said, "Everybody but you. You have nothing to worry about." There was a silence for a few seconds and then everybody started laughing including Betty and the boss.

Accidents, Fatal and Non-Fatal

A shipyard is one of the most dangerous places there is to work.

Accidents were a frequent happening at all the yards I worked at. In one five year period, six men died. Two men in separate accidents died as a result of falls. Two men were crushed in the cabs of their cranes in two unrelated accidents. Both cranes fell into building basins. One crane cab was about 110 feet over the basin floor when it fell. Another man was crushed when a four ton plate rolled over him. A young man was crushed when a bulkhead fell on him. The tragic part is in all the above accidents, carelessness was to blame and all the accidents should never have happened. In some cases, the men involved could have averted the accidents if they had been careful. Many other fatal accidents happened in the years I worked at other yards.

We were all told to report the smallest injury to our bosses, but if we reported all the injuries to the boss (sprains, contusions, cuts, scrapes, burns, material in the eye, etc.) he had to report to Personnel. Then, you would be branded as accident prone.

Some guys were accident prone and others were not. Most of my workers would report injuries to me, as their immediate supervisor, and ask me not to make a written record of the injury as they did not want to be reported to higher management. The idea was if the injury progressed and became worse, I would have a record of it. The reasoning behind this was the company would often suspect the injury had happened somewhere else other than the yard. If there was no report on, say, Monday and then Friday a man reported he had a back injury from Monday, the workmen's compensation company would not want to pay workmen's comp.

A man did not want to be branded as accident prone. If I did not tell him to go to First Aid and the injury grew worse, then I would be caught in the middle. Most men were conscientious and did not want to stop work for a small cut; others were macho and would not go to First Aid for anything less than a broken leg unless ordered to. There were others who would go for any reason and come back to work two or three hours later. It got so bad the company installed a time clock at First Aid. An injured employee was required to get his time card before going to First Aid and then punch his time card upon arrival there and when he left.

About 200 feet from where we worked, the company maintained hundreds of bottles of various gases; acetylene, argon, propane, oxygen and other flammable gases. In this area there was a building where gases were combined and the bottles were filled with various highly explosive gases. This building was as big as a large two story house.

Around supper time one night, the yard fire truck and city fire trucks showed up to fight a fire in this building. Judging by the billowing smoke, it soon became apparent that there was a substantial fire. Outside, there were various storage tanks holding thousands of gallons of highly explosive liquids. We all became worried about a major explosion. I talked to our boss about it and we discussed where we could go to shield ourselves from flying gas bottles or a massive fireball. I always thought this boss was a turkey and wouldn't have enough sense to come in from the rain. Our conversation proved my earlier suspicions. He said we had nothing to worry about and to keep working out in the open. I asked him if he had any idea of the danger this fire put us all in. He didn't have a clue. I told him I was going to stand behind a thirty foot tall ninety ton unit until the fire was put out. He threatened me with a chit and then told me he was going to call the second shift superintendent. All this idiot seemed to care about was production and the heck with us and our safety. I told him to call the super and mentioned that he had more brains than this boss. Then he really got mad and he threatened to fire me. As soon as I got behind the unit, my whole crew followed suit. Then all the welders, riggers, burners, and other personnel in the immediate area joined us, including their bosses. Our stupid boss stood right out in the open and played the part of macho man.

Finally, one of the welding bosses coaxed him to get behind the unit. The yard super drove by and saw about forty men all standing around doing nothing and stopped and came over to inquire about all these men standing behind the unit. My boss jumped forward and said, loud enough for all of to hear, "With the bad fire going on and the potential for gas bottles becoming missiles, I ordered the men to get behind this unit for safety's sake." The super said, "Wise thinking. Glad to see you practicing safety and thinking of your men."

One non-fatal accident had the potential of being much worse than it actually was. About six men were in a warming shack on a cold day. The riggers were using a crane lifting a heavy piece of steel weighing about 20 tons. It was about 30 feet high and 25 feet wide. When it was 25 feet off the ground, the cable connecting it to the crane snapped. The steel plate fell and struck a tall, heavy, portable steel staircase nearby. This toppled over and just missed the warming shack. The men in the warming shack ran outside when they heard all the noise. One man tripped and fell. He received some contusions and abrasions. This accident, like many others in the shipyard, could have been much worse.

The lengths some people would go to get out of a difficult job were funny and, sometimes, almost tragic. When they got a difficult job, some guys would suddenly get sick and tell the boss they were going home. One man called home and told his wife to call the yard and tell him the water pipes had burst.

One day we saw a lot of smoke billowing out of a hatch on the main deck up by the bow. A short time later, the yard fire engine showed up and after two hours, the smoke stopped and the engine left. By this time, the shift was over. I found out later that somebody had set a rubbish container on fire way down in the bilge of the ship. The man did it on purpose so he would not have to stay there and work on a rough job.

One tragic accident I remember involved two men working from a crane bucket. A crane bucket was also called a safety box. It was steel, five foot square, and had a solid bottom. The sides were four feet high with a safety rail around the perimeter. It was used to work on the side of the ship or other high areas. People would climb into the box and the box would be connected to the crane with a cable. Each individual in the box was required to wear a safety belt with snap attached to the rail on the safety box. Many men would wear the safety belt, but would not snap it onto the safety rail. These two men did not attach their snaps to the rail. The crane hoisted them off the ground about eighty feet into the air and over to the job. The job was completed and they were being lowered to the ground when the operator lost his brakes on the hoisting mechanism on the crane. The box started to fall quite fast. The brakes caught on the hoist and the box stopped short. One man was able to hang on but the other man was thrown out of the box and fell to his death. This was an accident that could have been averted by wearing a safety belt and having it properly attached to the rail on the box. Safety boxes were always dangerous to the men in them and sometimes the people on the ground.

Another type of box that was frequently passed overhead in our area was called a scrap box. These boxes were about eight feet long, four feet wide, and about two feet deep. All four sides of the box were closed in. After the unit was cleaned, a crane would lift it out with four cables attached to the four corners of the box. After a unit was finished, a scrap box would be lowered into the unit and laborers would fill it with debris which would consist of planks, paper bags, welding wires, and various pieces of steel weighing up to, maybe, 200 or 300 pounds. One yard

I worked in used boxes with one end open which made it much easier to dump. When it was dumped, two wires would be removed from the open end and the box's contents would fall into the scrap truck. One day, one of these boxes with the one open end was being lowered into a scrap truck. A rigger was in the back of the truck under the box when the load shifted and a jagged piece of steel weighing about forty pounds fell out with the pointed end down. The poor rigger didn't stand a chance. The pointed end punctured his hard hat like a hot knife going through butter and split the man's head almost in two. After that, all the boxes with open ends were brought in to the shop and the open ends were closed in.

One night, a man disappeared in the steel mill. The chief in charge of security told me they had been looking for him for hours with no luck. Security went out to the parking lot where this worker usually parked and his auto was still there. His time card had not been punched out. The mystery deepened. This man was a good worker with a good work history.

He had a responsible job running a large conveyor belt which stretched on for hundreds of feet. Steel plates eight to ten feet wide by up to forty feet long would roll by his machine to be delivered to another area. They moved on steel rollers about three inches in diameter and about twelve feet across. The plates rolled along slowly about the same pace a person walked. Sometimes when you walked by the plates would be rolling slowly along and other times they would stop for about an hour or so. The whole roller assembly was carried on a platform about two feet off the floor.

Right over the conveyor belt was a walkway only about three feet off the floor. This walkway was to save a person from walking hundreds of feet out of the way. There were signs posted telling people not to use the walkway when the belt was moving plates. The people in this area didn't pay any attention to the signs and would cross regardless of whether the plates were moving or not. Some fools would even walk on the moving plates rather than walk one hundred feet or more to the stairway over the plates. This particular night about four forty foot long by eight foot wide plates had rolled past the missing worker's station and then stopped at the other end because they were not ready for them on that end. After looking for him for hours, somebody looked where nobody else had—under the conveyor belt. There he was. The company figured the missing worker must have slipped on the walkway and fell onto the conveyor rollers just as the plate came along. Four plates, each weighing 12,800 pounds, had rolled over him pressing his body down into the rollers. The massive plates continued rolling until some-one on the far end shut the conveyor down. He was probably under the plates for hours. My friend, the second shift security chief, was the man who found him and said it was the worst accident he had ever seen. The corpsman said he probably died almost instantly as the first plate drove his body into the rollers.

After that, guard rails were installed on both sides of the walkway. Within a few weeks of the accident, fools were once again walking on and over the moving plates.

Lack of heat can be deadly, too. I would much rather work outside in cold temperatures than in unheated, clammy, damp shops. One of the shops I worked in was unheated. When I commented to the foreman about the lack of heat in the building, he said lack of heat was partially responsible for causing a horrendous accident and death. Just then we walked by a huge multispeed drill press. He said the press had killed a man the previous month. He said nothing more about the accident, but I noticed the drill press had been freshly painted. The levers and controls were bright red.

After working in the shop for a while, a co-worker told me about the accident. It had been a very cold day and the man had on a huge winter coat with loose sleeves. He was drilling holes in a plate at low speed and reached from one side of the machine to the other to speed up the drill. The drill bit caught his jacket sleeve and pulled his arm into the drill. Nobody in the immediate area heard anything. A co-worker walked by the drill which was over in the corner and noticed something strange whirling around. He stopped the machine and what he saw spinning was a man's arm torn off at the shoulder with the sleeve still caught on the drill bit.

The safety department reconstructed the accident and surmised that the worker had been dragged into the drill when he reached across to speed up the bit. His body was about twenty feet away and judging from the injuries to his body, they figured the body must have rotated many times with the motor at high speed until his arm separated from his shoulder and flung him about twenty feet away from the machine. He was DOA at the hospital from loss of blood and shock. It's terrible that people have to die before management will add safety features to machines that are potential killers.

Many companies complain about the Occupational Health and Safety Administration (OSHA), the government agency that mandates safety in the work place. Some things OSHA orders companies to do seem rather stringent, but there is no doubt they have saved many a life.

In the steel mill, various small plates, stringers, angle bars, and T bars are formed and fitted together to make different shaped sub-assemblies. A young worker had attached a small come-along to a six foot high T bar which is shaped like a T with the cross of the T always on top. This six foot high T bar weighed about 1200 pounds and had been set up on a sub-assembly with temporary braces. Everything holding the T bar up was tack welded in place by the previous shift. The young semi-skilled worker was trying to pull the bar up to a plumb vertical position to secure it before welding it down on the sub-assembly. He pulled too far with the come-along and the tack welds on the six foot T bar's braces broke. The assembly came over on him with the half inch thick by twelve inch wide T landing on his chest like a huge paper cutter, almost cutting him in two at the chest. The men rushed over and lifted the plate off him. His chest had been crushed and he was dead in a matter of minutes. What a terrible shame to see a young man with a wife and baby killed by a needless accident.

One winter, we were working aboard a ship in one of the basins. There were stagings built by the carpenters about every eight feet from the bottom of the basin right up the side of the ship to the main deck. Sometimes the stagings continued right up the side of the deckhouse to the bridge. On this ship, the bridge was 159 feet ABL (above base line or the bottom of the ship). The carpenters were taking down the staging before supper. During supper, a terrible snow and ice storm started. We went to work in a shop for the rest of the night. After supper, the carpenters were given the option of going home or working in the ice and snow. Most of them went home, but a few stayed. They would climb out on the staging with a chain and wrap it around a plank. Then they would step on to the adjacent plank and signal the crane operator to lift the plank that was wrapped in chain. A dangerous job in broad daylight that was made even worse after dark and absolutely treacherous in a snow storm. They should never have been out working in that weather. Our jobs were much less dangerous and we had been put into a shop for the night.

One carpenter was working with another carpenter who was landing the planks on the basin floor. Nobody knows what happened, but they figured the first carpenter must have stepped onto ice and fell. From where he was working, he fell over 100 feet to the basin floor. He must have bounced off many steel braces on the way down. He, too, was DOA at the hospital.

We had two 50 ton revolving cranes mounted on railroad tracks on either side of our building basins. The height from the roadway with the railroad tracks to the crane cab was about 65 feet. Approximately fifteen feet had been added to the bottom of these cranes so they could reach the new modern, higher ships we were building. The railroad tracks went all the way down the roadway adjacent to the building basins, about 900 feet, to the water's edge. Each of the cranes had about 100 foot long booms and because the cranes themselves could revolve, they could cover a wide area. The building basins were about 150 feet wide. Each crane could easily reach to the middle of the basin. This way we had four cranes servicing the basins.

I came to work one night and noticed one of the two cranes was missing. I walked over to the edge of the basin and looked down to the bottom. There lay the remains of the missing crane. It was unrecognizable other than it had been painted bright yellow. The night before, on the third shift, the crane picked up a heavy unit and swung it over the basin. Nobody but the poor operator knows what happened. Apparently when the crane swung the unit over the basin, the weight of the unit pulled the crane into the basin. The crane cab was about 125 feet over the basin floor when it fell. Lying on the bottom of the basin floor was a jumbled mess of yellow tangled steel. This was one boom we would never be able to repair.

The company also used cranes on rubber. These were cranes with telescoping booms and four huge rubber tires. We have all seen those types of cranes being moved on the highway. They were used all over the yard and were able to go anywhere. They were especially handy getting into areas where the big revolving cranes could not be utilized.

There were extendible hydraulic legs on all four corners of these types of crane. The legs are extended and placed on the ground when the crane needs to lift. When the legs are used this way they stabilize the crane and keep it from tipping over. If the load on the crane is to be swung 180 degrees to the other side, it is mandatory that the legs are extended and on the ground. A crane of this type was sometimes used at the edge of the basin to lift smaller items in or out of the basin. This way, the large revolving cranes could be utilized for heavy lifts without being tied up making small lifts.

One year we were out on strike for about three months. During this time, the company hired non-union scabs and also used management people to run equipment and keep the work moving. Our regular crane operators were out on strike with us when a crane on rubber was making a small lift at the edge of the basin. It toppled 65 feet down to the basin floor with the operator in the cab. I have often wondered whether the operator extended the legs before he made that fateful lift. He, too, was DOA at the hospital.

For a few years I erected steel at the yard on the second shift. We would erect as much steel on the second shift as possible so the first shift would have work when they came in. It was a dangerous job as pieces of steel did occasionally drop off the cranes. We used a tool called a grab to move much of the steel. It operated like a vise grip tool, clamping onto the steel and biting into the steel. When there was ice on the steel, the tool would sometimes not hold. We always tried to stay out from under the steel when we moved it. The bad part was we had to be under the steel to grab it when the crane lowered it down to us.

On windy days the work was even more dangerous because plates of steel would swing around in the wind when they were picked up. Some of these plates were as large as ten feet by forty feet and weighed many tons. Sometimes the crane operators would lower them and nudge them up against a unit to stop them from swinging. I got a lesson one night on what not to do with a swinging plate. We worked around one eight foot by thirty foot plate all night waiting for the wind to go down. The day shift foreman said to definitely get this plate in place before we went home. Finally, about 11:00 PM, the wind died down and we picked up the plate. When the crane swung it over to us, the wind picked up again and the plate started swinging back and forth. Like a fool, I grabbed it and thought I would be able to stop it from swinging. NO WAY! It pushed me backwards and I jumped about ten feet off the unit to the ground. If there had been a bulkhead behind me I would have been squashed like a fly. After I got back up on the unit, the crane operator lowered it down and when it touched the unit, it stopped swinging. Then we grabbed it and laid it down flat on the unit where it was supposed to go.

Fires on board ship were a common occurrence and there was the potential for someone to be trapped by the smoke in an inaccessible area. When I first started working in shipyards, the Brooklyn Navy Yard in New York had a tragic fire in which a score or more yard workers died. Staging caught fire on board an aircraft carrier and the victims died from smoke inhalation because they could not leave the ship fast enough. A short time later, I was working in the lowest level of the bow of a cruiser. It was down about eighty feet from the main deck and the only access was from the main deck. The whole bow was very heavily reinforced with vertical and horizontal bulkheads about every two feet. It took about ten minutes to go from the main deck to the bottom. I never have suffered from claustrophobia, but when I was down there working, I did a lot of thinking about the aircraft carrier fire and what would happen in a fire on this ship.

Some of the areas we had to work in were very small and it always seemed like the boss would put the biggest guy on the smallest job. We had to work down under the engine room on one job. Most ships, especially warships, have an inner bottom. This is a bottom within a bottom. It took us quite a while to crawl into the area through many manholes and down many passageways. All the while on our hands and knees dragging our tools and a welding line and the burner's lines for his torch. If it was not for these lines, we would have had a hard time finding our way out of this maze.

On this job, after using the burner's torch for a short time, we had to get out for a breath of air. We had burned up all the oxygen with the torch and the temperature was up around 150°. I never realized how good fresh air was. The yard supplied many different types of respirators for different jobs. This was one time when we should have had an independent air supply. These were available and were used by various trades. The only thing wrong with it was the hassle of getting the equipment and setting it up. We figured we would only be down there a short time and wouldn't need it. This is how accidents happen.

Carriers

After running out of Revolutionary War battle names, the navy seemed to have no rhyme or reason as to how they named new carriers. Battleships were still named after states and cruisers after cities. Some carriers were named after prominent people, like the *Cabot* or *Hancock*; others were named after insects, like the *Wasp* or *Hornet*.

The *Wasp* was built in Quincy in 1940 and sunk by the Japanese in 1942. The Quincy-built *Lexington* was also sunk in 1942.

In 1942, we needed a morale booster in the United States. The Japanese were kicking our butt in the pacific. That year, the Germans sunk well over 600 of our ships in the Atlantic.

The story of the naming of the *Shangri-La* was certainly a morale booster. The navy and the army air corps cooperated in a very unusual bombing mission. It was a top secret mission and only the top brass knew what was going on. A famous army air corps pilot by the name of Colonel Jimmy Dolittle was picked to lead the mission. Pilots were hand picked volunteers and trained for months for this mission not knowing what they were training for or where they were going. The mission was to bomb the Japanese home islands.

Sixteen B-25 land based bombers were loaded on to the carrier *Hornet*. The plan was for the *Hornet* to steam to approximately 450 miles of the coast off Japan and launch these 16 bombers and bomb Japan. When the carrier was about 650 miles off Japan it was spotted by Japanese fishing boats. Dolittle and his raiders were forced to take off 200 miles further out than had been planned. Each plane was given an extra 50 gallons of fuel and took off from the carrier's heaving deck. Dolittle took off first and when he became airborne, he still had 100 feet of carrier deck left, much to everyone's surprise.

Sixteen B-25s made it to Japan and bombed targets in Tokyo, Yokohama, Nagoya, and Kobe. The planes were all supposed to land in south central China, but that was socked in by weather. They had to fly well into China and most crews bailed out before they ran out of fuel. One plane did land intact in Russia and its crew was interned by the Russians. They bribed a Russian guard and made it home.

After this raid, the Japanese were horrified. The bombers hadn't done much damage, but the Japanese had been told by their rulers that American planes would never bomb the home islands. The biggest part of the whole mystery for the Japanese was where had these land based planes come from. They knew we did not have any land bases close enough to Japan to be able to reach Japan by air.

They sent agents and spies all over the world to try to find our new secret air base. President Roosevelt got a big kick out of the Japanese trying to find out where our new secret air base was. He got on the radio and told the world in one of his famous fireside chats that these planes had come from our new secret base called "Shangri-La".

The Japanese then set out agents trying to find our new base on "Shangri-La", wherever that was. In honor of that story, the new carrier *Shangri-La* was launched. The Dolittle raid on Japan was a huge morale booster in the United States and as a result of it, Jimmy Dolittle was promoted to the rank of brigadier general and awarded the Congressional Medal of Honor.

In the Battle of the Coral Sea the Japanese sunk the carrier *Lexington*. She was built in Quincy in the 1920s and was the second big carrier built for the Navy and launched shortly after the Navy's first big carrier, the *Saratoga*.

The shipyard workers in Quincy were shocked to find out their magnificent carrier had been sunk by the Japanese. At the time (1942), Quincy was building two new carriers for the Navy: the *Cabot* and the *Bunker Hill*. The Quincy workers petitioned the Navy to change the name of the new *Cabot* to the *Lexington* to honor their sunken ship. The Navy went along with the name change and the new *Lexington* was launched in 1943.

The new *Lexington* had a glorious record in WWII and served with distinction. She was one of the first Essex class carriers to have the new angled deck put on her after WWII. She served in Pensacola with the fleet until 1991. She was 48 years old when she was retired in 1991 and is presently on display as a museum ship in Corpus Christi, Texas. In the year 2003 she will be sixty years old. Another well built Quincy masterpiece. *Does Quincy build great ships, or what?*

Boston Navy Yard

I first started working at the Boston Naval Shipyard when it was still in the hands of the Navy. Seeing we were not old Naval Shipyard workers, they stuck us with some awful jobs. We were sometimes given dirty and undesirable jobs. One in particular involved getting down into the bottom of the aircraft carrier *Lexington and* cutting an eighteen inch diameter hole down through the engine room grating, the inner bottom and the bottom of the hull. Three different levels in all. The holes had to be cut at a fourteen degree angle off centerline on the port side. They were going to lead to a new inlet for sea water to the air conditioning system. My helper and I spent the better part of a morning finding the correct location. We crawled down under the engine room grating into the inner bottom and then down into the bilge. The bottom of the ship had about four inches of ice in it. After chipping out the ice, we laid out our eighteen inch hole. By this time, it was time to go home. We told the boss on the way out of the shop that we needed a burner the following morning to cut the holes.

The following morning, we told him again. For three days we told him three times a day we needed a burner. We would sit in the corner of the engine room out of sight every day and wait for the burner that never appeared. We figured as long as we told the boss about our need for a burner, we would just sit there and wait. After three days of this it got very boring. We would spend the day sleeping and reading. One man would sleep while the other read. The man who was reading was supposed to keep an eye out for the bosses or any navy brass that came through our area. My partner became very engrossed in his book and never even noticed the naval officer appear until it was too late. I was sound asleep.

Next thing I felt someone shaking me and woke up to find myself looking at a naval officer's uniform. He wanted to know what we were supposed to be doing. I told him what our job was and showed it to him. We was understandably quite upset and wanted to know why we were not working. I explained that we were waiting for a burner and could not do any more work without a burner. He asked how long we had been waiting for a burner. I blurted out, without thinking, that this was our fourth day of waiting. Boy, did he get agitated then! He came about two feet off the deck, jumping up and down, demanding to know how often we had asked our boss for a burner. I told him three times a day. He took down our badge numbers and disappeared. Within fifteen minutes, he was back with a burner and our boss who was furious that we had told the officer we had been waiting for a burner for four days. The next day, I was given a job up on the flight deck working with a burner cutting out and replacing old rusty foundations. The temperature was about ten degrees with a 25 MPH breeze. This was punishment duty for getting caught sleeping, a real no-no at a shipyard. The consequences would probably have been worse if we had not told the officer we had been waiting four days. The officer had said he didn't blame us for being bored and at least we were on the job. From then on, we got excellent burner service.

Working on navy ships did have compensations for us yard birds. Usually they were completely heated and their crews were still on board. On the second shift, we used to go down to the galley at coffee time. The cook would put out all the food that had not been consumed that day for the crew to snack on and always a pot of hot coffee. There was always some delicious pastries or cake besides the meat and vegetables. A big change from the cold, clammy dark ships that we usually worked on.

One of the warmest, most comfortable coats made is a Navy watch coat, also known as a Pea Coat. These are highly prized by shipyard workers. If you can find them in Army and Navy stores, they are expensive even for used ones. On one destroyer we worked on, we used to walk by the quartermaster's compartment every day. The door was made out of heavy mesh with a small opening at the top. Hanging over in the corner was a rack of brand new watch coats. We tried the door every night and it was always locked. One night, my partner got hold of a piece of 1/2 inch electrician's pipe about fourteen feet long and bent a hook on the end of it. The following night, he poked it over the top of the door and snagged two coats in short order. They were both large ones. Made to order.

A few months after I came to work at the Navy yard, the president decided to close the Boston Naval Shipyard. Most people figured it was because Massachusetts was the only state that did not vote for him. Senator Ted Kennedy and Speaker Tip O'Neill were no help at keeping the Navy yard open. At the time, the government was encouraging anybody who had enough years in government service to retire. Many workers did this and left early with full pensions. The shop I worked in quickly ran out of work but nobody was laid off. Everybody started working on home projects and goofing off. When a boss did come up with a job, everybody volunteered to help the person who got it. During this time, many fine weather vanes, spears, crossbows, car ramps, etc., were turned out at the Boston Naval Shipyard. In our shop, we had an automatic burning machine that would cut any shape that was drawn on paper and transfer it to a series of six cutting torches.

Behind our shop was a big field. One day, we drew a horseshoe on paper and soon had fabricated three pairs of horseshoes. We quickly had a great horseshoe tournament going. The boss broke it up and confiscated our horseshoes. As fast as he confiscated them, we made new ones. After about ten pairs, he finally gave up.

A short time later, they transferred most of us to the only remaining ship left in the yard. There were so many men that had quit or retired that there were not enough people left to finish the ship on time. Within a week, they ordered us to work twelve hour shifts. We worked from seven at night to 7:00 AM. Nobody wanted to get laid off as winter was approaching. Most of the men dragged out the work hoping the work would last till spring. The poor boss was frantic trying to get people to work harder.

All of us used to go to coffee about midnight. There were no coffee machines in the area so we would all get in one car and go to downtown Boston. We usually visited the Combat Zone in downtown Boston and stopped at one of the strip shows. After that, we drove to an all night Hayes Bickford for coffee and donuts. We would arrive back at the yard about 2:00 AM and put in an appearance on the job, making sure the boss saw us. About 3:00 AM people would sneak off to their cars in the parking lot for a nap. Usually, a short time later there would be a tap at your car window by the boss. Poor guy, he had an awful time getting people to stay on the job. He was a new boss who planned on staying in civil service after the yard closed. His intention was to get a bosses job at either the Norfolk, Virginia or the Portsmouth, New Hampshire naval shipyard. He was trying to establish a reputation as a boss that got a lot of work done. We were all yard birds whose main goal was to make it through the winter without getting laid off. Most of us had no intention of transferring to another naval yard after this yard closed. Every night it was the same routine. Every night people parked their cars in different places hoping the boss would not find your car and disturb your nap. This went on all winter and we were all laid off in the spring.

Some of the workers were offered jobs on the U.S.S. *Constitution,* which was built in 1797. She is the famous "Old Ironsides" berthed at the Boston Naval Shipyard. At the time, she was being completely rebuilt for the bicentennial by the U.S. Navy. She is the oldest commissioned war ship in the U.S. Navy. Some of the yard birds took this assignment, but most of us took our layoffs. I took a layoff because there was only four foot height between decks and the working conditions were extremely cramped for a six foot three inch guy.

Soon after, a private contractor leased part of the yard and started doing repair work on ships. Much of the work was on naval ships and was similar to the work that had been done when it was a naval yard. Many of the laid off workers were hired to work there. The company that leased the yard had very little equipment of its own. However, much of the equipment they had was leased and inadequate for the job. There was no union and many of the workers were doing jobs they had no training in. Now, a shipyard is a dangerous place at the best of times, but with inadequate equipment and unskilled help, it is treacherous. About this time, most of us found other jobs.

On the bridge of most naval ships there is a pair of very powerful binoculars. One day one of the yard birds was scanning the rooftops of the city with the binoculars and spotted two young ladies sunning themselves on a roof with no tops on. Before long, there was a crowd waiting to use the binoculars. An officer came along and broke up the crowd. From that day on, anybody passing the bridge on a sunny day stopped to have a look with the binoculars.

Sometimes I wonder how the ships we worked on could pass the Coast Guard inspections. One 110 foot ferry was in such poor shape and badly rusted out that I put a two pound hammer through the hull with just moderate pressure and this was below the water line. This ship carried passengers up and down the harbor every day. We often had to do repair jobs on these vessels, but it was difficult to put on a patch. We were supposed to cut out all the rusted bulkhead until we ran into sound steel. Sometimes this was impossible as there was no sound steel to tie into anywhere on the bulkhead. Fortunately, this rust bucket only operated in the harbor and never ran into any stormy weather or rough seas. We used to say the only thing holding them together was paint.

One particular ship I remember was a small naval vessel of about 300 feet. It came in for a complete refit. New deck houses, new engines, and all. Included in the job was a sandblasting and painting of the bottom. The total job was in the millions. The sand blasters started blasting the bottom and went right through because a lot of the bottom only had 1/4 inch of good steel left in it. This tub was about forty years old and the navy was spending all this money on it! Why spend millions on old rusting hulks? Hopefully, one of these days we will stop patching these old rust buckets and build new ships before it is too late.

Another hulk we worked on was a maritime ship for one of the New England states. This was another forty year old rust bucket used to train cadets on. Its bottom was as bad as some of the ferries. The sad part was cadets regularly went on cruises to Europe in her. I would not have gone down the coast in her. How she ever passed her annual inspection was a mystery to everyone who worked on her and as far as I know, she still goes to Europe on her summer cruise every year. The big oil companies usually sell a tanker to a foreign company after about twenty years, but the navy just keeps patching their old rust buckets.

<u>*Strikes and Layoffs*</u>

Shipbuilding contracts usually ran for three years. During the first year of most contracts the union members would receive a large raise. During the second and third years of the contract, the raises would be smaller. By the end of a three year contract, the workers always figured they were entitled to a hefty raise on the next contract. The company always thought different. Once, at the end of a three year contract, the union made a mistake of accepting a five year contract. At the end of this five year contract, the yard was the lowest paid in the United States. We always felt that we should be the highest paid yard as the area that the yard was located in had almost the highest cost of living in the continental United States.

So, there were frequent strikes at our yard. Most were lengthy, three months or longer. If the company had many ships under construction and more orders on the books it was sometimes a short strike. If the company had little work, the strike could be lengthy. The company and the union would start negotiating months before the contract ran out. The workers would always be kept in the dark as to what was going on. If it was in the spring or summer time, a lot of the yard workers wanted to go out on strike. They would vote for a strike unless the company offered a tremendous contract. Many of these workers were single and some had a part time job. All of them wanted the summer off. When a strike was called, it was always the same story at the yard. The first week or so there would be mass picketing. The company lawyers would go to court and get an injunction to stop the mass picketing. Until the company could get this injunction, the strike pickets would surround all the gates to the yard and nobody would be let in or out of the yard.

During one lengthy strike, the company became desperate to get scabs into the yard. Vans with blacked out windows were bringing the scabs in every day but they had to run the gauntlet of the picket lines. Picketers would spit at the vans and once in a while a stone would bounce off the vans. Good thing there was not a supply of stones nearby.

Somebody found out the company was going to start bringing in scabs by boat. Word got out about this and men were volunteering to ride "union gun-boats" to stop the scab boats. It looked like the harbormaster, the city police boat, and maybe even the coast guard would get involved. Fortunately, this did not happen, but I heard some bosses left the yard by boat.

People who stayed in the yard when the strike started would be locked in. Any scabs who tried to get through the gate ran the risk of serious injury from the picketers. Serious incidents happened at these strikes. Many times picketers would be arrested for disorderly conduct or assault and battery, but most of the local police were sympathetic to the yard workers. Some of them had relatives working at the yard or had even worked there themselves.

Along with the violence, a lot of funny things happened. One such incident involved the yard superintendent and a picketer. It was on the second day of a strike. Hundreds of strikers were at the main gate blocking the entrance when the yard superintendent arrived in his chauffeur-driven limousine. The police cleared the picketers away from the gates, but just as the limousine pulled up to the gate, a striker got past the police and jumped up on the hood of the limousine and started doing a dance on the hood. Everybody in the crowd gave the dancer a big hand. The police tried to grab the dancer but he jumped down from the car and disappeared into the crowd.

At one of these strikes, there were 500 or more strikers milling around the main gate and police were on hand to control the crowd. The company had secured a court injunction which forbade mass picketing at the gates to the yard. All that was allowed was an orderly picket line of about 8 to 10 men. This time, the yard was empty. The company wanted the bosses back in the yard. The bosses and other management people were supposed to go to work and get production going again on the ships. This included the women that worked in the offices. A rumor spread at the main gate that the bosses were going to enter the yard. Soon, bosses started arriving in large numbers. They formed on one side of the street. The strikers all ran across the street and blocked the gate. The police stood by and watched. The bosses crossed the street and tried to push their way through the crowd of strikers. A lot of pushing and shoving went on. No violence at all. I was pushing as hard as I could against a boss with my back to the man. I was still pushing against the boss when I heard a familiar voice say, "Back off Dave". It was a boyhood buddy I was pushing against. We both had a good laugh over that one.

Finally, the bosses retreated back across the street. Again, they crossed the street and tried to enter the yard again. Again much pushing and shoving. They retreated again. They had been told by the front office that they were to report to work, but most of the bosses did not want to enter the yard. Most of them had been hourly paid union workers. They were only following orders. Most of them did not want to see a strike. However, if the union won a large raise through a strike, then the bosses got a large raise too.

The following day more police were at the gates. This time, the police escorted the bosses into the yard. After that the large crowd of strikers dwindled daily. Then the company ran ads in the papers and started hiring scabs who were bussed into the yard in vans with the windows blacked out. They received extra pay to work in the yard during the strike.

After the strike was over, these same scabs who chose to remain in the yard were treated badly by the workers. Once a man became a scab, he was a marked man in the yard. When the word got out that an individual was a scab, nobody would work with him. Things were made so rough for him that most quit rather than take the verbal and physical abuse. A few of them were threatened and a few were hurt in mysterious, strange accidents. Some of them found their tool boxes broken into. Many of them found their cars vandalized in the parking lots. Within a year after the strike was over, most of the scabs had quit the yard. A few that were left were promoted into management.

Whenever a contract between the union and the company was about to run out, there were many rumors about what the union demands were and what the company was offering. The union would hold meetings with each trade in the yard. Each trade would state its demands for a new contract. Workers on the second shift would often go to the union meetings at supper time. If a worker stayed to the end of the meeting, he would probably arrive back at work an hour late from supper.

When the meetings were at the end of a contract, they often ran longer than a regular meeting. One night, near the end of a particular contract, a group of workers and me went to one of these meetings. Suppertime was from 7:30 to 8:00 PM. The union bought a few cases of beer as an incentive to get the workers to attend the meeting. We all stayed for the beer. At 9:00 the meeting finally got over. At 10:00 PM we all returned to the yard, arriving back about 10:30 PM. The guard would not let us in the gate. He said he had orders from the second shift super to hold us at the gate till he arrived. Before we left at suppertime, we all tried to find the boss to tell him we were going to a union meeting and would be back late. We had not been able to find the boss, so we told our co-workers to tell the boss that we would be late coming back after supper.

The super arrived at the main gate and we told him our story. He asked why we hadn't told the boss we were going to a union meeting. We told him we had tried but could not find him. We also told him we told our co-workers to tell the boss after supper that we would be back late from supper as we were going to a union meeting. The super told us we were all suspended pending investigation. He said that our boss said he had six men missing from his crew after supper. Our boss said that no one had told him we had gone to a union meeting. After much discussion and a few phone calls, our boss finally admitted that he had been told we were going to a union meeting. The super told us he would not suspend us, but we were all going to get a chit. He told us all to go back to work.

We called for our shop steward to protest the chits. The steward showed up on the job and told us to take the chits and the next day, he would have them all torn up. A chit consisted of four copies. One for the employee, one for the union, one for personnel, and one for the workers department office. The boss made out the chits for the six of us and handed them to us and walked away. The union steward asked for mine. He took one look at it and smiled. He asked for the other chits and when he had them all, he laughed and said, "That stupid boss gave everybody a chit and gave everybody all four copies." He gave us all back our chits and we all tore them up and threw them away. We were all laughing so hard that the boss came back and asked us if we thought a chit was a laughing matter. We all acted very serious and played the role of model employees.

After he left, we all went back to work and soon word had spread to the whole crew about the useless chits. That was one of the best laughs we had in a long time. The boss never did figure out why we were so happy about receiving chits. If he did, he was too embarrassed to ever admit the stupid mistake he made.

This boss was typical of many of the bosses in the yard. He had even taken the bosses job at a reduction in pay over what he had been earning as a worker. When a union member took a job in management, he lost all his seniority in the union. If he did not stay in management and wanted to get back into the union, he started at the bottom with no seniority. Many excellent qualified men who wanted to advance into management did not mainly because of this reason.

We had a boss who was constantly coming around and watching us. He would never say a word, just stand there and watch. We found out one day he did not like dirty stories or dirty jokes. A short time later, he was watching two men working. One man started telling the other man a dirty joke. The boss turned on his heel and left. Word quickly spread to the whole crew that a good way to get him off your back was to just start talking dirty. Soon even men who never told dirty jokes or stories would start talking this way when the boss came around. It worked every time.

Another boss we had was a real grouch. One day he came to work and was in a very good mood. We all noticed a smell of liquor on his breath. A short time later, one of the guys was at a barroom at suppertime and noticed the boss there having a beer. After supper the boss was in a good mood again. The following night when he came around checking on the crew, a co-worker offered him a beer. He looked around to see if anyone was watching and said yes. Soon he was stopping by every night for a beer. Within a couple of months, he was bringing in a six pack every night and we had the best natured boss in the whole yard. Sadly, the affable boss was soon fired.

For many years, you could almost count on a strike when a contract was completed. It sometimes seemed like a strike was inevitable at the end of a contract. Months before the end of a contract the union negotiating team would have meetings with management representatives. Both sides would present their demands and conditions for the new contract. Initially both sides would be far apart. After many meetings, both sides would usually be close to a contract. The company would tell the local press what a great contract they had offered the workers and that the new contract would make the workers some of the highest paid shipyard workers in the country.

The union would hold a mass meeting of workers at a city stadium and a vote would be taken to take or reject the proposed contract. A typical vote would go something like this: a union stooge would stand up and say, "I propose we do not accept the company's offer". Another stooge would stand up and say, "I second the motion." Then the union official would say, "We have a motion made and seconded. Any discussion?" If anybody wanted to speak they were usually not recognized. Occasionally they would be allowed to speak. Then the union official would repeat, "We have a motion made and seconded. Any more discussion?" There never was any more discussion. The motion would then be put to the floor for a voice vote of ayes and nays. The ayes would always win and the next thing we knew, we would be leaving the stadium scratching our heads and saying, "What happened? Why are we out of a job and on strike?" Almost every time we all agreed the people wanting to accept the contract would be in the majority but the nays would be much louder than the ayes. Some union officials liked to have a strike. This made them big wheels and often got their names in the newspapers.

Sometimes the strikes dragged on for months. A person could not collect unemployment compensation while on strike and people living from paycheck to paycheck would really be hurting very quickly. Some workers went right on welfare, veteran's aid, food stamps, etc.

The company and union would then have more meetings and sometimes the company would rescind the previous offer and offer a less lucrative offer. Both sides would then dig in their heels and try to wait the other side out. The poor workers would get by any way they could. Nobody would hire a worker on strike knowing he would leave his new job when the strike was over.

Some strikers would drive cabs, paint houses, dig clams; anything to turn a buck and survive. Some would not lower themselves to accept any kind of welfare, veteran's aid or food stamps. Some would take any handout they could and between handouts and part time jobs, they would make out quite well.

People with any brains and knowing the past history of the yard would put aside money every month for those inevitable strikes or layoffs. I got a kick out of the new term for layoffs when it was first coined: RIF (reduction in force). It still meant no paycheck. With this new language, job titles often got changed, even garbage men became known as "sanitary engineers".

We had regular customers at my parents' store who bought cigarettes, newspapers, soda, chewing tobacco, etc. When a strike or a layoff was underway, those customers would say, "I am going to get another job and never go back to the yard. I've had it with that place!" Usually, a few months later, after the strike was over, they would stop in to our store and admit they were back at the yard. For people with specialized skills, such as shipfitter, pipe welder, burner, there weren't many other job opportunities locally and most did not pay as well as the yard, especially with overtime.

One strike dragged on all summer and into the fall. Along about October, I had depleted most of our rainy day money and was concerned about the approaching long, cold winter. I decided I should at least inquire as to what I had to do to get food stamps. Men I worked with had been getting some form of aid since we first went out on strike.

I drove an older car, lived in a small house and lived modestly. Some of my co-workers on welfare lived in big houses and drove big cars, smoked cigarettes, and drank at least a six pack a day. What a shock I got when I inquired about food stamps. The office clerk told me I was not eligible. I asked why I was not and I was told I had too much money in the bank. I asked the clerk, "How about if I use the money in the bank for a down payment on a new car. I will then have payments of hundreds of dollars a month on the new car." She said that would be fine. Then I would be eligible for food stamps. This bugged me no end. Here I had saved for a rainy day and this was my reward. If you ask me, it's a lousy system! Fortunately, the strike was soon over. I never did get that new car. I was too busy saving for the next rainy day at the shipyard.

Launchings, Then and Now

There are basically two ways to launch a ship: stern first or sideways. Both methods were done on wooden launchways. In the case of a ship launched stern first, the launchways were built up wooden inclined ramps at least as long as the ship being built and usually only about twenty to twenty-five feet wide even for a ship with a one hundred foot beam (width). Later launchways were built out of concrete. Both the wooden and concrete launchways were similar to modern day boat ramps.

In some cases, the launchways were two inclined ramps parallel to one another and separated by about fifteen feet. Some were one solid wooden ramp about twenty to twenty-five feet wide.

The launchways were built during the lowest tides of the year and extended many feet out to where deep water was at high tide. When the ship was launched at high tide, the underwater extension on the launchway carried the ship to deep water before she floated free of her poppets (cradles).

In the old days, ships were built from the ground up on these launchways. When shipbuilding first started, the construction of the human body was copied and the same terminology was used: backbone (keel); frames (ribs); shell plates (skin). A small poppet would be put on the launchway and then the ship's keel (backbone) would be placed on the poppet. As more pieces of the keel were laid down, end to end, additional poppets were placed under these keel pieces. Attached to the keel at right angles were the ship's frames (ribs). These frames would be spaced out for the entire length of the ship. On warships, the frames were closer together for strength. On commercial cargo ships, they were usually spaced further apart. Stringers (or longitudinals) would be placed starting at the keel, running the full length of the ship. These full length longitudinals would extend from the bow (front) of the ship to the stern (back of the ship). There would be dozens radiating out from the keel up to the main deck of the ship. The longitudinals were placed in slots on the frames and welded to the frames. This kept the frame spacing accurate. Attached to these frames and longitudinals would be steel shell plates (skin) of the ship. This method of shipbuilding was used for thousands of years all over the world, right up until roughly WWII.

As the ship was being built on the launchway, more and more materials would be needed to support the thousands of tons of steel. The poppets only extended out about ten to twelve feet on either side of the keel. A ship might extend maybe another forty feet beyond the keel on either side. Additional braces in the form of 12X12 by 20 or 30 or 40 foot timbers would be placed under and along side the ship in an upright position to steady the ship on the ways. As the ship grew larger and heavier, more of these timbers would be added for support.

As the ship grew, horizontal stagings would be installed completely around the ship from about ten feet off the ground right up the sides of the ship about every eight feet. These would extend as high up as the ship went, sometimes over 150 feet from the ground. After the exterior of the ship was completed, all of the staging had to be removed before the ship could be launched.

There were multiple stagings around the stern of the ship. Welded onto the stern were many pads with holes in them. Chain falls were attached from these pads to lift the massive bronze propellers onto the shafts of the ships. Aircraft carriers usually have four propellers. The overhead cranes lower the props onto the ground. (Overhead cranes could not be utilized to raise the props as they are attached up under the stern forward of the steering rudder.) Chain falls are then attached to the props and the props weighing hundreds of tons are raised by hand with the chainfalls and slid onto the shafts.

After the hull is complete, including the rudder and propellers and the main machinery (boilers, generators, and engine room equipment), the ship is launched and then moved to the outfitting piers. After the tow to the outfitting piers, all exterior components are added to the ship. It might take from a few months to a year to complete the ship.

She then goes out on sea trials which usually last a few days. On sea trials all the ship's machinery is tested and put through its paces. The anchor is lowered and raised dozens of times. The engines are run wide open and all the owners' specifications must be met. If the navy said they wanted a cruiser that would steam at 30 knots, 27 knots is not good enough. The ship must meet or exceed all specifications in the contract. If, after the initial trials, the ship meets or exceeds her specs, she comes back to the yard flying a broom in the rigging. She is said to have made a clean sweep of her trial run. This is a happy day for the yard management, the workers, and her owners. If the broom is not in the rigging, the ship has failed to live up to her original specifications. The problems must be corrected and she goes back out on trials again. Some ships go out a few times before all the problems are ironed out.

I remember one very expensive trial for the yard on a huge tanker. There was a problem out at sea on trials and they were delayed coming back to the yard. When they did finally get back, the tide was dropping instead of rising. The decision was made to ease her into thirteen slip. When the tugs started pushing her into thirteen slip, she touched bottom. The decision was made to use her own power to help push her into the slip. The propellers started turning and mud was churned up from the bottom. At this time, she should have been backed out and put at a pier with deeper water.

Tugboats cost hundreds of dollars an hour. There were four tugs aiding her and she had a yard crew on her earning overtime. Each additional hour would cost the company thousands of dollars. It would have taken another hour or two to pull her out of thirteen slip and move her to a deep water slip. All the while, the tide was dropping at the rate of almost two foot an hour. There was a good chance she might have grounded, sticking out into the channel for hours until the next high tide. This would mean the tugs and men would have to stand by for hours, waiting for the high tide. The decision was made to get her into thirteen slip. The propellers really started churning and mud completely stained the water. She dragged bottom all the way into the slip. At the time, it seemed like a wise decision. After she was tied up, divers were sent down to check the bottom and her propellers. After the divers' inspection, it was decided to put her in dry dock and further check her propellers.

Upon further inspection of her propellers, it was decided to remove them and have them refurbished by the manufacturer. A ship's propeller is made out of bronze and is relatively soft compared to steel. It turned out to be a very serious mistake to push her into thirteen slip. In the long run, it would have been much cheaper to pull her out and put her at a deep water pier even if hours were wasted waiting for the incoming tide.

When launch day is approaching, the ways are greased. Various materials can be used: beeswax, lard, and tallow are some of them. The greasing is done the day before and if it is warm, sometimes ice is put over the grease to keep it firm until just before the launching.

On the big day, the millwrights and carpenters are there before dawn for the final steps. Most of the stagings had already been removed as well as most of the big timbers (uprights) supporting the sides and stern of the ship. Then, all other timbers are removed. The wedges are driven and the ship is ready to go. Just before the sponsor breaks the bottle of champagne, the last timbers holding the ship are released. Not visible to the crowd under the reviewing stand is the hydraulic ram at the bow. If the ship does not start moving within seconds the hydraulic ram gives the ship a push to start her moving. Some yards have a powerful tug standing by with a rope on the stern of the ship to pull her into the water if necessary.

Before launch day, a huge pile of old anchor chains weighing hundreds of tons would be laid down in the shape of a horseshoe in front of and alongside the ship. The amount of chain laid down would depend on the size of the ship. The heavier the ship, the more chain would be laid down. Sometimes the chain would be laid down in separate piles, maybe two huge piles on each side of the ship

These chains were called drag chains. One end would be attached to the ship. As the ship slid down the ways, it would drag the chains with it. This would slow down the momentum of the ship and eventually stop it dead in the water. This area of the Fore River was only deep (dredged) out about 2,000 feet from the launchways. After that, it was only six feet deep or less at low water. Without these drag chains, the ship would end up going across the river into the mud. This did happen more than once and it was very embarrassing for everyone concerned.

In 1940 Quincy built the new aircraft carrier *Wasp* for the United States Navy. Apparently she didn't have enough drag chains and went right across the river into the mud and stayed there for a while. It took many tugs straining and a high tide to free her from the mud. The old time yardbirds (shipbuilders) and the navy personnel said that was a bad omen. They are a superstitious bunch and all agreed this was a terrible start for this new carrier.

Two years later, in 1942, she was sunk by the Japanese navy. I would imagine when she was sunk by the Japanese the yardbirds all agreed it was because of the bad start. The ninth *Wasp*, CV-18, was started in Quincy in 1942 as the *Oriskany*. After the previous *Wasp* was sunk the *Oriskany's* name was changed to honor the sunken *Wasp* on 13 November 1942. She was launched on 17 August 1943. She had a glorious combat record in WWII earning eight battle stars during that conflict. She was homeported in Boston for many years. During that time, she was used to recover the *Gemini IV* astronauts in the Atlantic after touchdown in 1965. Her last home port was Quonset Point, Rhode Island. She was decommissioned in July, 1972.

Launchings always seemed like more fun when I was a boy. We usually skipped school and walked up the bridge to watch or "borrowed" a rowboat to watch from the river. Back then, the coast guard never seemed to bother us and we used to get close to the launching. I was out in the river on my own boat for the launching of the *Kalamazoo* in 1971 and the coast guard kept us about one half mile away. It was not anywhere near as exciting as when I was a boy.

The last launching at Quincy was the navy oiler *Kalamazoo*, AOR-6. She was delivered to the navy in 1972. Launchings were always a big event at the yard. Sometimes the company would invite the families of the workers into the yard to celebrate the big day. A band would play and a minister would pray over the ship and wish her a safe and long life. Refreshments would be served and at the appointed time, the ship's sponsor would say words like, "I christen thee *"Lexington"* and may all who sail with her be safe." At the launching of the *Thomas W. Lawson* in 1902, the local newspaper estimated there were 20,000 people watching the launching of the world's only seven masted schooner.

Quincy built more destroyers than all other U.S. shipyards combined. Destroyer launchings were especially exciting. They are a lot lighter than, say, a tanker and also a lot narrower. A tanker enters the water at a rather stately gait: slow and ponderous. A destroyer practically runs in like she's ready to show you how fast she can go.

The destroyers used to be launched near the Fore River Bridge. The launchways were close enough to the bridge so that people on the bridge could get a good view. During the war years, watching destroyer launchings was almost a weekly event. Sometimes three were launched in a month.

The concrete footings for the cranes in this area were right at the water's edge. At high water, the footings on some of the cranes were partially submerged. During one destroyer launching, some men were standing on the footings. They were about two feet above the water. When the ship goes down the ways, it pushes a wall of water in front of it. This pulls the water away from the shoreline and makes a big wave radiating out from the stern of the destroyer. After the ship slows down, the water comes rushing back into the shore in the form of a large wave. The faster the ship enters the water, the bigger the wave and the faster it moves. On this occasion, when the wave came back into shore, it washed men off the concrete footings. Fortunately, there were no injuries other than to their pride.

The end of an era happened in 1971 when Quincy launched its last ship, the *Kalamazoo*. The last launchway was turned into a building basin. Building ships on launchways was expensive for many reasons, especially the poppet (cradle and shores). One of the worst problems for the machinists and shipfitters was the angle of the ship as it sat on this inclined launchway. In front of each ship is a sign giving the hull number and the declivity of that particular ship. The declivity was usually between three sixteenth of an inch per foot up to maybe three eighths of an inch per foot. What this referred to was the angle of this ship and her decks on the ways. For example, on a ship with three-eighths declivity, for every one foot of ship length the ship angled down, bow to stern, three eighths of an inch, two feet of the ship went downhill three quarters of an inch. Three foot of ship sloped down one and one eighth of an inch.

All machinery on a ship sits on a foundation and the foundation must be level before it is welded down. After it is welded, the machinery is either welded or bolted to the foundation. Every machinist or shipfitter working on foundations had various declivity boards. They were usually the same length as a two foot level. A three eighth declivity board would have a three quarter inch angle (slope). A three sixteenth declivity board would have a three-eighths of an angle slope. When laying out machinery foundations, these declivity boards would be held under the level. This would give you a level mark on the foundation before it was installed on the ship. You might work on two ships side by side. One might have declivity of three sixteenths and one might have declivity of three eighths. You always had to make sure you were bringing the right declivity board for the ship you were working on. It was a big pain in the neck and made your job more diffi-cult and time consuming.

Ships built in basins were built on level basin floors and as a result no declivity boards were necessary to install foundations. Then, it was much quicker and cheaper to lay out foundations.

Henry Kaiser, amongst others, pioneered side launching. With this method, large ships could be built in narrow rivers. The ship would be built parallel to the water instead of at right angles like traditional stern first launchings. Ships would slide into the water but would enter sideways. In addition to the large wave, there would also be an enormous splash. The ship would look like it was going to tip over and sink when she first hit the water. After almost tipping over, the ship will right itself onto an even (level) keel.

Shipyards were reluctant to construct building basins initially because of the tremendous construction cost. Besides, if the yard already had building ways they had used for fifty years and they were sufficient, how could they justify the expen-diture required to construct building basins.

Bethlehem Steel built three building basins in Quincy in the 1950s including the mammoth number seven basin. Number seven was over 1,000 feet long and dwarfed the adjacent number six and number eight basins. The huge tanker *Manhattan* was built in number seven basin and took up all available room. There was hardly any room to build the staging alongside the ship and in front of the bow. She was the heaviest ship in the world when her keel was laid in the late 1950s.

The basins were built at high cost. Imagine a hole about 65 feet deep, 1,000 feet long, and 150 feet wide. Just the excavating cost alone would run in the millions of dollars. Then this enormous hole had to be lined on three sides with concrete. The bottom had to be exceptionally thick concrete to hold the weight of mammoth ships. After the concrete was poured on the sides, bottom, and front, massive steel I beams were installed along with thousands of feet of additional bracing. The basin floors were approximately thirty-five feet below MHW (mean high water, or average high tide). There were enormous steel folding gates at one end of the basins. Ships could be built in these basins with a lot less bracing holding up the ships.

After the hull was complete and most of the machinery and the deckhouse were installed, the ship could be floated out (launched). This was nowhere near as dicey an operation as launching a ship down sliding ways. Launches on sliding ways were, at best, expensive and dangerous operations, but floating a ship out was nowhere as much fun to watch as a launching.

The night before a float out, huge round gate valves, about 24 inches in diameter, were opened below MHW on the gates. Torrents of water would rush in. Bethlehem Steel would put dye in the water rushing into the basin. The torrents initially dropped about twenty feet to the bottom of the dry basin. It was fascinating watching the colorful red, white, and blue water fall into the basin. In a matter of hours, the basin would be flooded. When the height of the water in the basin equaled sea level, the gates would be lowered. Tug boats would then tow the ship out of the basin and tow it to an outfitting pier.

After the ship left the basin, the massive gates would be brought back up and then the huge pumps would pump the basin dry. Floating a ship out was about as exciting as watching the tide come in.

One night, the basin next to us which held a mammoth LNG, was flooded. Periodically, my helper and I would look into the basin to see how much water was there and to see if the ship was floating. My helper was a new hire and couldn't figure out how something that was made of steel and weighed thousands of tons could float. As the water rose higher and higher in the basin, he commented, "Do you think it will float?" During supper, we walked over to look and he realized the main deck was now well above ground level where previously it had been much lower. He was amazed.

We were always curious to see how many species and numbers of fish would be left flopping on the basin floor. Sometimes just a few fish, but oftentimes thousands of fish. If the fish were smelt or flounder, men would go into the basin at lunch time to pick up as many as possible. Then the laborers would enter the basin to clean the floor and stack the hundreds of keel blocks that floated free when the ship initially floated.

The Best Yard: Diversity

Along with the usual tankers and freighters, Quincy built battleships and submarines. Before Electric Boat in Groton, Connecticut even had their own shipyard, Quincy built dozens of submarines for Electric Boat. Subs were also built for Japan and a battleship for Argentina.

We not only built more destroyers than the total output of all other U.S. shipyards, combined, we also built the first and second nuclear powered surface warships for the U.S. Navy: the heavy cruiser, *Long Beach* and the destroyer, *Bainbridge*. The yard set a record on destroyer construction which will probably never be equaled. From April 1918 to May 1920, a period of 25 months, Quincy delivered 71 destroyers to the U.S. Navy. This was about three ships a month for two years. Sometimes two a week were delivered. This was long before the so called automation we have today. Was this a shipyard, or what?

Quincy also turned out numerous aircraft carriers. Quincy-built LNGs (liquefied natural gas) were the most successful LNGs ever built in the world. Up until that time, the 120 foot aluminum spheres were the biggest objects ever made of aluminum. No where in the world had aluminum that thick been prefabricated and welded into a sphere. The company that subcontracted the spheres in South Carolina went bankrupt trying to build them. Fifty of these huge spheres had to be built. They weighed an incredible 800 tons each. These 120 foot spheres had to be walked out of the building and loaded onto the *Hercules* barge and shipped up to Quincy, almost 1,000 miles away.

The most incredible thing to me about the LNGs was the temperature of the gas that these ships carried. It was natural gas, which has to be frozen down to about 250 degrees below zero before turning into a liquid. It was pumped as a liquid into these ships at about 260 degrees below zero. The ship traveled all the way from Indonesia to Japan and the gas had to be kept at this temperature. Talk about machinery! We used to say these ships had the biggest air conditioning units any one ever designed and built.

The Quincy-built Lykes Brothers sea-bee barge carrying ships were the first ever built. The elevators on these ships were the biggest ever installed on any ship, including the huge new aircraft carriers.

The first collier (coal carrier) built in the U.S. in forty years was built in Quincy. She could completely unload herself with no shore side cranes. During WWII this yard and its Hingham, Massachusetts subsidiary built hundreds of ships for the U.S. Navy, including a battleship, six carriers, over twenty cruisers, dozens of destroyers, and hundreds of landing craft, including LSTs (landing ships tank, 320 feet), LCIs (landing ship infantry), and various other landing craft.

What made this yard unique was its engineering department. While other yards would specialize in one type of ship, for instance, carriers or destroyers, Quincy would tackle anything. When ship owners, including the U.S. Navy, wanted a new type of ship or a private owner wanted a new unique ship, Quincy would be called on to design it and usually built it. They were even proposing building huge oil tanker subs to carry the North Slope oil under the ice to a warm water port rather than build the Alaskan pipe line. It was the Quincy-built U.S.S. *Manhattan* that was converted into the world's largest icebreaker for this mission. She made the voyage, carrying one symbolic barrel of oil, through the Northwest Passage to prove icebreaking tankers could carry the North Slope oil to a warm water port

The last ships built at Quincy were the MPS (maritime prepositioning ships) rapid deployment vessels. Those, too, were a completely new type of ship and the U.S. government decided again, as they had in the past, to award the contract to the yard with the best capability to build them. The MPS were 673 feet long and weighed in at 41,700 tons, almost three times as big as a WWII supertanker.

Needless to say, the MPS cargo carrying capacity is awesome. They have seven vehicle decks and can accommodate about 1400 vehicles. Additionally, they can carry 522 twenty foot cargo containers. Their liquid capacity is 200,000 gallons of gasoline; 540,000 gallons of diesel; 855,000 gallons of jet fuel; and 82,000 gallons of potable water. Each ship can produce 36,000 gallons of potable water a day from her two distilling plants. Each ship carried enough material and supplies to support 3,000 men for a month.

Any good sized shipyard can build small freighters. More engineering is needed to build oil tankers. Some yards specialized in a few kinds of ships. Quincy built them all; more different types and highly specialized ships than any other yard. When times were tough, Quincy workers even built automobiles (called Fore Rivers) and texas towers.

End of an Era

Quincy delivered six maritime pre-positioning ships between February 1985 and May 1986. These were 673 foot long ships. The deckhouses on these ships were completely assembled in the basins. When the first one was lifted onboard the MPS ship *John P. Bobo*, it weighed an amazing 1,120 tons. At the time, this was the heaviest lift ever in a U.S. shipyard. These were the last ships built at Quincy and so ended the best shipbuilding yard in the United States, and maybe the world.

Before the MPS ships left, Quincy bid on more ships. These included container ships and survey ships for the navy. No new contracts were awarded, though, so General Dynamics had no choice than to close the Quincy yard in 1986. After 102 years, the yard that was started by Alexander Graham Bell's assistant was closed.

Lots of reasons were given for the yard closing. The main reasons given over and over in various newspapers and editorials were labor unions and management problems. Another reason given was foreign competition. I do not believe these were the principal reasons. Local and state representatives, the mayor, the governor, and other officials all said that if the Quincy yard was to prosper, a new, wider or a high level bridge must be built. These statements were repeatedly reported in the local press. I believe the main reason was that the Commonwealth of Massachusetts and the federal government did not care enough about the shipbuilding industry. Quincy could have stayed open if our senators, representatives, and our president did something. In the years the shipyard was in trouble, the speaker of the house was Tip O'Neill, our senator was Ted Kennedy, and our president was John Kennedy. John McCormick was speaker before Mr. O'Neill. The city of Quincy and the city of Boston are next to each other and all of the above individuals were from the Boston area.

A few hundred feet from the shipyard is a drawbridge with a narrow opening. Back in the 1950s, ship sizes started getting much bigger. When the *Manhattan* went out to sea, it barely passed through the opening. Ship owners were demanding larger and larger tankers and container ships. The navy wanted bigger carriers. Quincy could not bid on any of these ships because of the bridge.

Over the years, there was talk again and again about a new bridge. Way back in the late 1940s, one of our neighbors owned a big piece of vacant land near the yard. He charged shipyard workers a fee to park their automobiles there. When he was approached by a real estate company about selling his land for development, he said he was going to sell it to the state because the new bridge was about to be built and the state would need his land. Everyone knew that without a new bridge, the shipyard was doomed.

Bath Iron works in Maine kept on winning new contracts. The shipyards in Mississippi were awarded new contracts, including one to build two new American registered cruise ships for the Hawaiian Islands.

In the 1970s, President Nixon signed a bill to subsidize up to 300 new civilian ships to be built in the United States. The bill would allow U.S. ship owners to have their ships built in U.S. yards with subsidies to offset higher U.S. labor costs. Under this bill, the three Lykes Seabees were built in Quincy.

Japanese yards, too, have high labor costs. I believe that today U.S. yards would be competitive with the Japanese yards. In Operation Desert Storm, we found that much of our war material had to be shipped in decrepit old U.S. ships or ships owned by our allies. There are very few commercial ships left in U.S. registry.

President Clinton said about shipbuilding and the Quincy yard in particular, "Shipbuilding is one of the keys to America's national defense and helping our shipbuilders succeed commercially is an important goal of defense conversion." He also said, in 1993, "This administration is committed to preserving highly skilled American jobs and we believe that American shipbuilding can compete and win in world markets."

What happened to this promise in 1993? It has been stated also that wages at Quincy were not competitive with other U.S. yards. Many times, we were paid less than our principal competition, Newport News, and we were usually paid about the same as other U.S. yards. At the end of the three year contracts, we were usually the lowest paid.

In conclusion, I believe it was poor representation in Washington from our representatives as well as the fact that we had a bridge too small to allow VLCC's (very large crude carriers) and other large ships to pass through. Incidentally, the decrepit Fore River Bridge is finally being replaced. It was falling down and the state had no choice other than to replace it. This is like "Closing the door after the horse was stolen."

◆   ◆   ◆

In writing this book, most of the accounts were eyewitness and some were told to me by fellow yard birds. It may appear that work was hardly ever done. I would like to emphasize that when you have thousands of people working together, there will always be a few goof-offs, drunks, etc. The <u>vast</u> majority of people I worked with were decent, hardworking, industrious workers.

Credits

President Clinton's remarks: from a MARAD release dated December 18, 1997

Senator Kennedy's remarks: from a speech made at Fore River Shipyard, December 18, 1997

Senator John McCain remarks: quoted by the Associated Press on January 1, 1996.

Fore River Shipyard Production Records: compiled by Andrew Toppan and listed under his website, Haze Gray and Underway.

Aerial photographs of Fore River Shipyard showing LNGs and the Goliath Crane, courtesy of General Dynamics Corporation.

Aerial photograph of the U.S.S. Massachusetts underway, courtesy of the U.S.S. Massachusetts Memorial Committee, Fall River, Massachusetts, home of the "World's Largest Peacetime Navy". Six ships in all.

Photograph of the U.S.S. Lexington (the "Blue Ghost"), courtesy of the Museum on the Bay, Corpus Christi, Texas.

Photograph of the 2nd LT John P. Bobo passing through the Fore River Bridge, courtesy of Haze Gray and Underway. Used by permission of Andrew Toppan.

Photograph of the U.S.S. Salem (the "Sea Witch"), in Venice, Italy, courtesy of Seaweed Ships Histories, Sisterville, West Virginia. The Salem is the centerpiece of the U.S. Naval and Shipbuilding Museum at the Fore River Shipyard in Quincy, Massachusetts

Photograph of the battleship Rivadavia, courtesy of Haze, Gray and Underway

Photograph of the seven masted schooner, Thomas W. Lawson, courtesy of Haze, Gray and Underway

Photograph of tanker Manhattan, courtesy of Bethlehem Steel

Photograph of Watson's Bridge, courtesy of General Dynamics

The author also wishes to thank the countless friends, acquaintances and fellow yard birds who contributed to this book.

All other photographs were taken by the author.

APPENDIX

Fore River Shipyard Production Record

Part 1: Hull 100 through Hull 375

Hull 1376 through Hull 1397

(1884 through 1924)

This is a complete list of all Fore River Shipyard production, listed in order by Fore River hull number. Small repair or overhaul jobs that were not assigned hull numbers are not included. This listing includes the Quincy Fore River yard under the ownership of the Fore River Engine Co. (1900-1901), the Fore River Ship & Engine Co. (1901-1913) and Bethlehem Steel (1913-1963); also included are the original Fore River Engine Co. yard at East Braintree (1884-1903), and the Bethlehem Steel yard at Squantum (1918-1920).

This list was compiled and is maintained by Andrew Toppan, using sources listed at the bottom of the document.

The first column is the Fore River hull number, followed by a designation for the yard in which the ship was built, the vessel's name, the type/size/class of the vessel, the owner/customer for the vessel, the type of work done (new construction, overhaul, etc.), the date the vessel was delivered, and the fate or status of the vessel. For ships that remain in existence the current name is listed in the status/fate column; if no name is listed, the vessel retains its original name.

The yard designations are as follows:
EBr = East Braintree Yard, original yard of Fore River Engine Co.
Q = Quincy Fore River yard (main yard), under all corporate names.
S = Squantum Yard, WWI emergency annex to Bethlehem Quincy.

For conversions and reconditionings, the vessel's new name (at completion) is listed under "name", the original name and description are listed under "type", and the nature of the conversion is listed under "work type".

Fore River Shipyard Production Record

Hull	Yard	Name	Type/Descr.	Owner	Work Type	Delivered	Fate or Status
100	EBr	*Sally*	Yacht	Lyman	New	Unk.	Unknown
101	EBr	*Caprice*	Yacht	Robinson	New	Unk.	Unknown
102	EBr	*Eleanor*	Yacht	Clapp	New	Unk.	Unknown
			Lawrence Class				

103	EBr	*Lawrence* (DD 8)	(420 Ton) Destroyer	US Navy	New	7 Apr 1903	Scrapped 1920
104	EBr	*MacDonough* (DD 9)	*Lawrence* Class (420 Ton) Destroyer	US Navy	New	3 July 1903	Scrapped 1920
105	EBr	*Jule*	Yacht	J. Arthur	New	12 June 1899	Unknown
106	EBr	*Light Vessel No. 72*	113' Lightship (Diamond Shoals Station)	US Light House Service	New	13 Feb 1901	Discarded 1937
107	Q	*Des Moines* (C-15)	*Denver* Class 3rd Class Cruiser	US Navy	New	5 Mar 1904	Scrapped 1930
108	Q	*New Jersey* (BB 16)	*Virginia* Class Battleship	US Navy	New	12 May 1906	Target 5 Sept 1922
109	Q	*Rhode Island* (BB 17)	*Virginia* Class Battleship	US Navy	New	12 Feb 1906	Scrapped 1924
110	Q	*Thomas W. Lawson*	404' 7-Masted Coal Schooner	Coastwise Transportation Co.	New	10 Sept 1902	Wrecked 13 Dec 1907
111	Q	--	317' Carfloat	New York, New Haven & Hartford Ry	New	6 Dec 1902	Unknown
112	Q	--	317' Carfloat	New York, New Haven & Hartford Ry	New	6 Dec 1902	Unknown
113	Q	*William L. Douglas*	353' 6-Masted Coal Schooner	Coastwise Transportation Co.	New	11 Nov 1903	Unknown
114	Q	*Boston*	317' Freighter	New England Navigation Co.	New	16 July 1904	Scrapped 1934
115	Q	*Providence*	396' Coastal Passenger Steamer	New England Navigation Co.	New	21 Mar 1905	Scrapped 1938
116	Q	--	317' Carfloat	New York, New Haven & Hartford Ry	New	17 Nov 1903	Unknown
117	Q	--	317' Carfloat	New York, New Haven & Hartford Ry	New	12 Dec 1903	Unknown
118	Q	--	317' Carfloat	New York, New Haven & Hartford Ry	New	10 Feb 1904	Unknown
119	Q	--	317' Carfloat	New York, New Haven & Hartford Ry	New	10 Feb 1904	Unknown
120	Q	*Vermont* (BB 20)	*Connecticut* Class Battleship	US Navy	New	11 Feb 1907	Scrapped 1924

121	Q	*No. 3*	167' Tank Barge	Standard Oil Co.	New	23 Nov 1904	Unknown
122	Q	*No. 4*	167' Tank Barge	Standard Oil Co.	New	16 Dec 1904	Unknown
123	Q	*No. 1*	67' Submarine	Japanese Navy	New	5 Oct 1904	Discarded 1921
124	Q	*No. 2*	67' Submarine	Japanese Navy	New	5 Oct 1904	Discarded 1921
125	Q	*No. 3*	67' Submarine	Japanese Navy	New	5 Oct 1904	Discarded 1921
126	Q	*No. 4*	67' Submarine	Japanese Navy	New	5 Oct 1904	Discarded 1921
127	Q	*No. 5*	67' Submarine	Japanese Navy	New	5 Oct 1904	Discarded 1921
128	Q	*Octopus* (SS 9)	C-Class Submarine	Electric Boat Co. for US Navy	New	16 May 1908	Discarded 1920
129	Q	*Viper* (SS 10)	B-Class Submarine	Electric Boat Co. for US Navy	New	16 Oct 1907	Target 1922
130	Q	*Cuttlefish* (SS 11)	B-Class Submarine	Electric Boat Co. for US Navy	New	16 Oct 1907	Target 1922
131	Q	*Tarantula* (SS 12)	B-Class Submarine	Electric Boat Co. for US Navy	New	29 Nov 1907	Target 1922
132	Q	*Birmingham* (CS-2)	*Chester* Class Scout Cruiser	US Navy	New	10 Apr 1908	Scrapped 1930
133	Q	*Salem* (CS-3)	*Chester* Class Scout Cruiser	US Navy	New	27 July 1908	Scrapped 1930
134	Q	*Spray*	136' Trawler	Bay State Fishing Co.	New	6 Dec 1905	Unknown
135	Q	*Creole*	410' Passenger Steamer	South Pacific Co.	New	22 Dec 1907	Scrapped 1937
136	Q	*South Shore*	207' Coastal Passenger Steamer	Nantasket Beach Co.	New	16 June 1906	Wrecked 28 Apr 1928
137	Q	*Satilla*	313' Freighter	Brunswick Steamship Co.	New	10 Nov 1906	War Loss 7 Feb 1917
138	Q	*Ochmulgee*	313' Freighter	Brunswick Steamship Co.	New	4 Apr 1907	Scrapped 1929
139	Q	*Ogeechee*	313' Freighter	Brunswick Steamship Co.	New	29 Dec 1906	War Loss 29 July 1917
140	Q	*Ossabaw*	313' Freighter	Brunswick Steamship Co.	New	24 Feb 1907	Scrapped 1933
141	Q	*Everett*	400' Collier	New England Coal & Coke	New	19 Oct 1907	Scrapped 1948
142	Q	*Malden*	400' Collier	New England Coal & Coke	New	2 Dec 1907	Collision 17 Sept 1921
143	Q	*Melrose*	400' Collier	New England Coal & Coke	New	11 Jan 1908	Scrapped 1947
144	Q	*Altamaha*	313' Freighter	Brunswick Steamship Co.	New	30 Dec 1907	Barged 1924; Abandoned 1933

Fore River Shipyard Production Record, Part 1   Page 4 of 16

145	Q	*New England*	131' Lighter	New England Navigation Co.	New	2 Nov 1907	Unknown
146	Q	*Transfer No. 21*	125' Harbor Tug	New York, New Haven & Hartford Ry	New	19 Jan 1908	Unknown
147	Q	*Light Vessel No. 90*	135' Lightship (Hedge Fence Station)	US Light House Service	New	14 May 1908	Discarded 1955
148	Q	*Light Vessel No. 91*	135' Lightship (Relief No. 1)	US Light House Service	New	29 May 1908	Discarded 1963
149	Q	*Light Vessel No. 92*	135' Lightship (Relief No. 2)	US Light House Service	New	15 June 1908	Discarded 1954
150	Q	*Light Vessel No. 93*	135' Lightship (Swiftsure Station)	US Light House Service	New	6 July 1908	Discarded 1955
151	Q	*North Dakota* (BB 29)	*Delaware* Class Battleship	US Navy	New	10 Apr 1910	Scrapped 1931
152	Q	*Stingray* (SS 13)	C-Class Submarine	Electric Boat Co. for US Navy	New	16 Oct 1909	Discarded 1920
153	Q	*Tarpon* (SS 14)	C-Class Submarine	Electric Boat Co. for US Navy	New	14 Oct 1909	Discarded 1920
154	Q	*Bonita* (SS 15)	C-Class Submarine	Electric Boat Co. for US Navy	New	20 Oct 1909	Discarded 1920
155	Q	*Snapper* (SS 16)	C-Class Submarine	Electric Boat Co. for US Navy	New	22 Oct 1909	Discarded 1920
156	Q	*Narwhal* (SS 17)	D-Class Submarine	Electric Boat Co. for US Navy	New	7 Oct 1909	Scrapped 1922
157	Q	*Grayling* (SS 18)	D-Class Submarine	Electric Boat Co. for US Navy	New	11 Oct 1909	Scrapped 1922
158	Q	*Salmon* (SS 19)	D-Class Submarine	Electric Boat Co. for US Navy	New	1 Sept 1910	Scrapped 1922
159	Q	*General R. Anderson*	98' Harbor Tug	US Army	New	25 Jan 1909	Unknown
160	Q	*General R. Arnold*	98' Harbor Tug	US Army	New	29 Jan 1909	Unknown
161	Q	*General R.B. Ayers*	98' Harbor Tug	US Army	New	9 Feb 1909	Unknown
162	Q	*General J.M. Brannan*	98' Harbor Tug	US Army	New	13 Feb 1909	Unknown
163	Q	*General H. Brown*	98' Harbor Tug	US Army	New	20 Feb 1909	Unknown
164	Q	*General G.B. Getty*	98' Harbor Tug	US Army	New	1 Mar 1909	Unknown
165	Q	*General B. Jackson*	98' Harbor Tug	US Army	New	8 Mar 1909	Unknown
		General M.				19 Mar	

Fore River Shipyard Production Record, Part 1

166	Q	*Randol*	98' Harbor Tug	US Army	New	1909	Unknown
167	Q	*No. 54*	327' Carfloat	New York, New Haven & Hartford Ry	New	21 Nov 1908	Unknown
168	Q	*No. 55*	327' Carfloat	New York, New Haven & Hartford Ry	New	5 Dec 1908	Unknown
169	Q	*No. 56*	327' Carfloat	New York, New Haven & Hartford Ry	New	22 Dec 1908	Unknown
170	Q	*No. 57*	327' Carfloat	New York, New Haven & Hartford Ry	New	2 Jan 1909	Unknown
171	Q	*No. 58*	327' Carfloat	New York, New Haven & Hartford Ry	New	20 Jan 1909	Unknown
172	Q	*No. 59*	327' Carfloat	New York, New Haven & Hartford Ry	New	13 Feb 1909	Unknown
173	Q	*No. 60*	327' Carfloat	New York, New Haven & Hartford Ry	New	18 Feb 1909	Unknown
174	Q	*Transfer No. 22*	125' Harbor Tug	New York, New Haven & Hartford Ry	New	4 May 1909	Unknown
175	Q	*Perkins* (DD 26)	*Roe* Class (700 Ton) Destroyer	US Navy	New	15 Nov 1910	Scrapped 1935
176	Q	*Sterett* (DD 27)	*Roe* Class (700 Ton) Destroyer	US Navy	New	12 Dec 1910	Scrapped 1935
177	Q	*Aloha*	218' Yacht	A.C. James	New	11 May 1910	Unknown
178	Q	*Herman Frasch*	361' Bulk Freighter	Union Sulphur Co.	New	5 Apr 1910	Collision 4 Oct 1918
179	Q	*E-1* (SS 24)	E-Class Submarine	Electric Boat Co. for US Navy	New	13 Feb 1912	Scrapped 1922
180	Q	*E-2* (SS 25)	E-Class Submarine	Electric Boat Co. for US Navy	New	14 Feb 1912	Scrapped 1925
181	Q	*Walke* (DD 34)	*Pauling* Class (700 Ton) Destroyer	US Navy	New	18 July 1911	Scrapped 1935
182	Q	*No. 13*	128' Ammunition Lighter	US Navy	New	19 Jan 1910	Unknown
183	Q	*Miguelito*	131' Molasses Lighter	Porto Rico Merchantile Co.	New	29 Jan 1910	Unknown
184	Q	*Fifi*	150' Molasses Barge	Cuba Dist. Co.	New	31 Jan 1910	Unknown

185	Q	Graziela	150' Molasses Barge	Cuba Dist. Co.	New	31 Jan 1910	Unknown
186	Q	Santa Maria II	115' Molasses Barge	Columbus Dist. Co.	New	5 Feb 1910	Unknown
187	Q	Rivadavia	Rivadavia Class Battleship	Argentine Navy	New	27 Aug 1914	Scrapped 1956
188	Q	Currier	386' Tanker	Cuba Dist. Co.	New	15 Dec 1910	Scuttled 8 June 1944
189	Q	Foam	126' Trawler	Bay State Fishing Co.	New	14 Sept 1910	Unknown
190	Q	--	250' Carfloat	Pennsylvania RR	New	28 Dec 1910	Unknown
191	Q	--	250' Carfloat	Pennsylvania RR	New	17 Dec 1910	Unknown
192	Q	Sankaty	195' Coastal Passenger Steamer	New Bedford Steamship Co.	New	14 Apr 1911	Sunk 27 Oct 1964
193	Q	Ripple	126' Trawler	Bay State Fishing Co.	New	23 Dec 1910	Unknown
194	Q	New Orleans	315' Suction Dredge	US Army Corps of Engineers	New	4 Apr 1912	Unknown
195	Q	Crest	126' Trawler	Bay State Fishing Co.	New	29 Nov 1910	Unknown
196	Q	Henley (DD 39)	Monaghan Class (700 Ton) Destroyer	US Navy	New	5 Dec 1912	Scrapped 1934
197	Q	Newton	406' Collier	New England Coal & Coke	New	20 Nov 1911	Scrapped 1947
198	Q	K-1 (SS 32)	K-Class Submarine	Electric Boat Co. for US Navy	New	17 Mar 1914	Scrapped 1931
199	Q	K-2 (SS 33)	K-Class Submarine	Electric Boat Co. for US Navy	New	28 Jan 1914	Scrapped 1931
200	Q	Swell	129' Beam Trawler	Bay State Fishing Co.	New	29 Dec 1911	Unknown
201	Q	Surf	129' Beam Trawler	Bay State Fishing Co.	New	4 Jan 1912	Unknown
202	Q	Duncan (DD 46)	Cassin Class (1000 Ton) Destroyer	US Navy	New	30 Aug 1913	Scrapped 1935
203	Q	K-5 (SS 36)	K Class Submarine	Electric Boat Co. for US Navy	New	19 Aug 1914	Scrapped 1931
204	Q	K-6 (SS 37)	K Class Submarine	Electric Boat Co. for US Navy	New	5 Sept 1914	Scrapped 1931
205	Q	Nevada (BB 36)	Nevada Class Battleship	US Navy	New	11 Mar 1916	Target 31 July 1948
		Fulton	Fulton Class				

206	Q	(AS 1)	Submarine Tender	US Navy	New	2 Dec 1914	Discarded 1934
207	Q	*Nelson*	386' Tanker	Cuba Dist. Co.	New	17 Nov 1912	Scrapped 1958
208	Q	*Frieda*	314' Bulk Freighter	Union Sulphur Co.	New	19 Feb 1913	Torpedoed 20 Oct 1943
209	Q	*Richmond*	436' Tanker	Standard Oil Co.	New	23 Sept 1913	Scrapped 1949
210	Q	*No. 61*	342' Carfloat	New York, New Haven & Hartford Ry	New	14 June 1913	Unknown
211	Q	*No. 62*	342' Carfloat	New York, New Haven & Hartford Ry	New	9 July 1913	Unknown
212	Q	*Wave*	129' Beam Trawler	Bay State Fishing Co.	New	2 Sept 1913	Unknown
213	Q	*Billow*	129' Beam Trawler	Bay State Fishing Co.	New	15 Aug 1913	Unknown
214	Q	*Breaker*	129' Beam Trawler	Bay State Fishing Co.	New	26 Aug 1913	Unknown
215	Q	*Cushing* (DD 55)	*O'Brien* Class (1000 Ton) Destroyer	US Navy	New	21 Aug 1915	Scrapped 1936
216	Q	*No. 63*	342' Carfloat	New York, New Haven & Hartford Ry	New	12 Aug 1913	Unknown
217	Q	*No. 64*	342' Carfloat	New York, New Haven & Hartford Ry	New	1 Sept 1913	Unknown
218	Q	*Amolco*	329' Tanker	Boston Molasses Co.	New	25 Jan 1914	Scrapped 1953
219	Q	*L 1* (SS 40)	*L* Class Submarine	Electric Boat Co. for US Navy	New	11 Apr 1916	Scrapped 1922
220	Q	*L-2* (SS 41)	*L* Class Submarine	Electric Boat Co. for US Navy	New	11 Apr 1916	Scrapped 1933
221	Q	*L-3* (SS 42)	*L* Class Submarine	Electric Boat Co. for US Navy	New	21 Apr 1916	Scrapped 1933
222	Q	*L-4* (SS 43)	*L* Class Submarine	Electric Boat Co. for US Navy	New	4 May 1916	Scrapped 1922
223	Q	*M-1* (SS 47)	*M* Class Submarine	Electric Boat Co. for US Navy	New	14 Feb 1918	Scrapped 1922
224	Q	*Atlantic*	405' Freighter	J.S. Emery Co.	New	22 July 1914	Torpedoed 12 Sept 1917
225	Q	*Pacific*	405' Freighter	J.S. Emery Co.	New	29 Sept 1914	Lost 1/1921
226	Q	*Tucker* (DD 57)	*Tucker* Class (1000 Ton)	US Navy	New	10 Apr 1916	Scrapped 1937

148   THE SHIPYARD

		Destroyer					
227	Q	L-9 (SS 49)	L Class Submarine	Electric Boat Co. for US Navy	New	4 Aug 1916	Scrapped 1934
228	Q	L-8 (SS 50)	L Class Submarine	Electric Boat Co. for US Navy	New	2 Aug 1916	Scrapped 1922
229	Q	L-11 (SS 51)	L Class Submarine	Electric Boat Co. for US Navy	New	15 Aug 1916	Scrapped 1933
230	Q	H-11	H Class Submarine	Royal Navy	New	2 Dec 1915	Discarded 1921
231	Q	H-12	H Class Submarine	Royal Navy	New	2 Dec 1915	Discarded 1922
232	Q	H-13	H Class Submarine	Royal Navy	New	2 Dec 1915	Discarded 1949
233	Q	H-14	H Class Submarine	Royal Navy	New	2 Dec 1915	Scrapped 1925
234	Q	H-15	H Class Submarine	Royal Navy	New	2 Dec 1915	Scrapped 1925
235	Q	H-16	H Class Submarine	Royal Navy	New	7 Dec 1915	Discarded 1945
236	Q	H-17	H Class Submarine	Royal Navy	New	7 Dec 1915	Discarded 1945
237	Q	H-18	H Class Submarine	Royal Navy	New	7 Dec 1915	Discarded 1945
238	Q	H-19	H Class Submarine	Royal Navy	New	9 Dec 1915	Discarded 1953
239	Q	H-20	H Class Submarine	Royal Navy	New	9 Dec 1915	Discarded 1953
240	Q	--	H Class Submarine	Royal Navy	New	--	Cancelled
241	Q	--	H Class Submarine	Royal Navy	New	--	Cancelled
242	Q	Sampson (DD 63)	Sampson Class (1000 Ton) Destroyer	US Navy	New	24 July 1916	Scrapped 1936
243	Q	Rowan (DD 64)	Sampson Class (1000 Ton) Destroyer	US Navy	New	24 July 1916	Scrapped 1939
244	Q	Texas	432' Tanker	Texas Oil Co.	New	18 Feb 1916	Scrapped 1950
245	Q	New York	432' Tanker	Texas Oil Co.	New	9 Apr 1916	Scrapped 1950
246	Q	AA-1 (SS 52)	AA Class Submarine	Electric Boat Co. for US Navy	New	30 Jan 1920	Scrapped 1930
247	Q	Cubadist	406' Tanker	Cuba Dist. Co.	New	26 May 1916	Lost 2/1920
248	Q	Edward	456' Freighter	Edward F.	New	28 Nov	Collision, sunk

		Luckenbach			*Luckenbach*			1916	21 July 1939
249	Q	*Sucrosa*	406' Tanker	Cuba Dist. Co.		New		30 June 1916	Scrapped 1946
250	Q	*Isaac Peral*	*M* Class Submarine	Spanish Navy		New		25 Jan 1917	Hulked 1930
251	Q	*Julia Luckenbach*	456' Freighter	Edward F. Luckenbach		New		25 Jan 1917	Collision 23 Sept 1943
252	Q	*Mielero*	406' Tanker	Cuba Dist. Co.		New		14 Feb 1917	Sunk 26 Jan 1920
253	Q	*Pennsylvania*	432' Tanker	Texas Oil Co.		New		30 June 1917	Scrapped 1948
254	Q	*Virginia*	432' Tanker	Texas Oil Co.		New		29 July 1917	Scrapped 1947
255	Q	*Ingeniero Luis A. Huergo*	343' Tanker	Argentine Navy		New		30 Apr 1917	Scrapped 1960
256	Q	*O-3* (SS 64)	*O* Class Submarine	Electric Boat Co. for US Navy		New		14 June 1918	Scrapped 1946
257	Q	*O-4* (SS 65)	*O* Class Submarine	Electric Boat Co. for US Navy		New		28 May 1918	Scrapped 1946
258	Q	*O-5* (SS 66)	*O* Class Submarine	Electric Boat Co. for US Navy		New		8 June 1918	Scrapped 1925
259	Q	*O-6* (SS 67)	*O* Class Submarine	Electric Boat Co. for US Navy		New		11 June 1918	Scrapped 1946
260	Q	*O-7* (SS 68)	*O* Class Submarine	Electric Boat Co. for US Navy		New		4 July 1918	Scrapped 1946
261	Q	*O-8* (SS 69)	*O* Class Submarine	Electric Boat Co. for US Navy		New		11 July 1918	Scrapped 1946
262	Q	*O-9* (SS 70)	*O* Class Submarine	Electric Boat Co. for US Navy		New		27 July 1918	Lost 20 June 1941
263	Q	*O-10* (SS 71)	*O* Class Submarine	Electric Boat Co. for US Navy		New		17 Aug 1918	Scrapped 1946
264	Q	*K.I. Luckenbach*	469' Freighter	Edward F. Luckenbach		New		3 Feb 1918	Scrapped 1954
265	Q	*F.J. Luckenbach*	469' Freighter	Edward F. Luckenbach		New		28 Nov 1917	Scrapped 1951
266	Q			*Unknown*					
267	Q	*Katrina Luckenbach*	469' Freighter	Edward F. Luckenbach		New		18 May 1918	Scrapped 1953
268	Q	*George W. Barnes*	432' Tanker	Petroleum Transp. Co.		New		5 June 1918	Scrapped 1948
269	Q	*W.L. Steed*	432' Tanker	Petroleum Transp. Co.		New		9 Sept 1918	Torpedoed 23 Jan 1942
270	Q	*T-2* (SF 2)	*AA* Class Submarine	Electric Boat Co. for US Navy		New		7 Jan 1922	Scrapped 1930
271	Q	*T-3*	*AA* Class	Electric Boat Co.		New		7 Dec 1920	Scrapped 1930

		(SF 3)	Submarine	for US Navy			
272	Q	*Nantasket*	406' Freighter	Emergency Fleet Corp.	New	16 Oct 1918	Scrapped 1939
273	Q	*Cohasset*	406' Freighter	Emergency Fleet Corp.	New	30 Nov 1918	Scrapped 1937
274	Q	*Little* (DD 79)	*Wickes* Class Destroyer	US Navy	New	5 Apr 1918	Sunk 5 Sept 1942
275	Q	*Kimberley* (DD 80)	*Wickes* Class Destroyer	US Navy	New	27 Apr 1918	Scrapped 1922
276	Q	*Sigourney* (DD 81)	*Wickes* Class Destroyer	US Navy	New	14 May 1918	Scrapped 1947
277	Q	*Gregory* (DD 82)	*Wickes* Class Destroyer	US Navy	New	31 May 1918	Sunk 5 Sept 1942
278	Q	*Stringham* (DD 83)	*Wickes* Class Destroyer	US Navy	New	2 June 1918	Scrapped 1946
279	Q	*Dyer* (DD 84)	*Wickes* Class Destroyer	US Navy	New	1 June 1918	Scrapped 1936
280	Q	*Colhoun* (DD 85)	*Wickes* Class Destroyer	US Navy	New	23 May 1918	Bombed 30 Aug 1942
281	Q	*Stevens* (DD 86)	*Wickes* Class Destroyer	US Navy	New	23 May 1918	Scrapped 1936
282	Q	*R-1* (SS 78)	*R* Class Submarine	Electric Boat Co. for US Navy	New	16 Dec 1918	Scrapped 1946
283	Q	*R-2* (SS 79)	*R* Class Submarine	Electric Boat Co. for US Navy	New	24 Jan 1919	Scrapped 1946
284	Q	*R-3* (SS 80)	*R* Class Submarine	Electric Boat Co. for US Navy	New	17 Apr 1919	Scrapped 1948
285	Q	*R-4* (SS 81)	*R* Class Submarine	Electric Boat Co. for US Navy	New	28 Mar 1919	Scrapped 1946
286	Q	*R-5* (SS 82)	*R* Class Submarine	Electric Boat Co. for US Navy	New	15 Apr 1919	Scrapped 1946
287	Q	*R-6* (SS 83)	*R* Class Submarine	Electric Boat Co. for US Navy	New	1 May 1919	Scrapped 1946
288	Q	*R-7* (SS 84)	*R* Class Submarine	Electric Boat Co. for US Navy	New	12 June 1919	Scrapped 1946
289	Q	*R-8* (SS 85)	*R* Class Submarine	Electric Boat Co. for US Navy	New	21 Jul 1919	Target 19 Aug 1936
290	Q	*R-9* (SS 86)	*R* Class Submarine	Electric Boat Co. for US Navy	New	30 July 1919	Scrapped 1946
291	Q	*R-10* (SS 87)	*R* Class Submarine	Electric Boat Co. for US Navy	New	20 Aug 1919	Scrapped 1946
292	Q	*R-11* (SS 88)	*R* Class Submarine	Electric Boat Co. for US Navy	New	5 Sept 1919	Scrapped 1948
293	Q	*R-12* (SS 89)	*R* Class Submarine	Electric Boat Co. for US Navy	New	23 Sept 1919	Lost 12 June 1943

Fore River Shipyard Production Record, Part 1   Page 11 of 16

294	Q	*R-13* (SS 90)	*R* Class Submarine	Electric Boat Co. for US Navy	New	17 Oct 1919	Scrapped 1946
295	Q	*R-14* (SS 91)	*R* Class Submarine	Electric Boat Co. for US Navy	New	24 Dec 1919	Scrapped 1946
296	Q	*S-1* (SS 105)	*S-1* Class Submarine	Electric Boat Co. for US Navy	New	5 June 1920	Scrapped 1945
297	Q	*Lewis Luckenbach*	527' Freighter	Edward F. Luckenbach	New	8 May 1919	Scrapped 1957
299	Q	*Andrea Luckenbach*	527' Freighter	Edward F. Luckenbach	New	12 June 1919	Torpedoed 10 Mar 1943
299	Q	Unknown					
300	Q	*Lexington* (CC 1)	*Lexington* Class Battlecruiser	US Navy	New	--	Suspended 8 Feb 1922; Sunk 8 May 1942
1300	Q	*Lexington* (CV 2)	*Lexington* Class Battlecruiser	US Navy	Completion as *Lexington* Class Aircraft Carrier	14 Dec 1927	Sunk 8 May 1942
301	Q	*Bell* (DD 95)	*Wickes* Class Destroyer	US Navy	New	1 Aug 1918	Discarded 1936
302	Q	*Stribling* (DD 96)	*Wickes* Class Destroyer	US Navy	New	16 Aug 1918	Target 1936
303	Q	*Murray* (DD 97)	*Wickes* Class Destroyer	US Navy	New	20 Aug 1918	Scrapped 1936
304	Q	*Israel* (DD 98)	*Wickes* Class Destroyer	US Navy	New	13 Sept 1918	Scrapped 1939
305	Q	*Luce* (DD 99)	*Wickes* Class Destroyer	US Navy	New	11 Sept 1918	Scrapped 1936
306	Q	*Maury* (DD 100)	*Wickes* Class Destroyer	US Navy	New	23 Sept 1918	Scrapped 1934
307	Q	*Lansdale* (DD 101)	*Wickes* Class Destroyer	US Navy	New	26 Oct 1918	Scrapped 1939
308	Q	*Mahan* (DD 102)	*Wickes* Class Destroyer	US Navy	New	24 Oct 1918	Scrapped 1931
309	Q	*S-19* (SS 124)	*S-1* Class Submarine	Electric Boat Corp. for US Navy	New	16 Aug 1922	Scuttled 18 Dec 1938
310	Q	*S-18* (SS 123)	*S-1* Class Submarine	Electric Boat Corp. for US Navy	New	17 May 1922	Scrapped 1947
311	Q	*S-20* (SS 125)	*S-1* Class Submarine	Electric Boat Corp. for US Navy	New	25 Mar 1922	Scrapped 1946
312	Q	*S-21* (SS 126)	*S-1* Class Submarine	Electric Boat Corp. for US Navy	New	6 Sept 1922	Target 23 Mar 1945
		S-22	*S-1* Class	Electric Boat			

313	Q	(SS 127)	Submarine	Corp. for US Navy	New	4 Apr 1922	Scrapped 1946
314	Q	S-23 (SS 128)	S-1 Class Submarine	Electric Boat Corp. for US Navy	New	2 May 1922	Scrapped 1947
315	Q	S-24 (SS 129)	S-1 Class Submarine	Electric Boat Corp. for US Navy	New	3 Aug 1922	Destroyed 25 Aug 1947
316	Q	S-25 (SS 130)	S-1 Class Submarine	Electric Boat Corp. for US Navy	New	24 June 1922	Lost 2 May 1942
317	Q	S-26 (SS 131)	S-1 Class Submarine	Electric Boat Corp. for US Navy	New	18 Sept 1922	Collision 24 Jan 1942
318	Q	S-27 (SS 132)	S-1 Class Submarine	Electric Boat Corp. for US Navy	New	29 Nov 1922	Wrecked 19 June 1942
319	Q	S-28 (SS 133)	S-1 Class Submarine	Electric Boat Corp. for US Navy	New	14 Oct 1922	Lost 4 July 1944
320	Q	S-29 (SS 134)	S-1 Class Submarine	Electric Boat Corp. for US Navy	New	11 Dec 1922	Scrapped 1947
321	Q	Palmer (DD 161)	Wickes Class Destroyer	US Navy	New	22 Nov 1918	Mined & Bombed 7 Jan 1945
322	Q	Thatcher (DD 162)	Wickes Class Destroyer	US Navy	New	14 Jan 1919	Scrapped 1946
323	Q	Walker (DD 163)	Wickes Class Destroyer	US Navy	New	31 Jan 1919	Hulked 1939; Scuttled 28 Dec 1941
324	Q	Crosby (DD 164)	Wickes Class Destroyer	US Navy	New	24 Jan 1919	Scrapped 1946
325	Q	Meredith (DD 165)	Wickes Class Destroyer	US Navy	New	29 Jan 1919	Scrapped 1936
326	Q	Bush (DD 166)	Wickes Class Destroyer	US Navy	New	19 Feb 1919	Scrapped 1936
327	Q	Cowell (DD 167)	Wickes Class Destroyer	US Navy	New	17 Mar 1919	Scrapped 1949
328	Q	Maddox (DD 168)	Wickes Class Destroyer	US Navy	New	10 Mar 1919	Scrapped 1952
329	Q	Foote (DD 169)	Wickes Class Destroyer	US Navy	New	21 Mar 1919	Scrapped 1949
330	Q	Kalk (DD 170)	Wickes Class Destroyer	US Navy	New	29 Mar 1919	Scrapped 1945
331	Q	Belknap (DD 251)	Clemson Class Destroyer	US Navy	New	28 Apr 1919	Scrapped 1946

332	Q	*McCook* (DD 252)	*Clemson* Class Destroyer	US Navy	New	30 Apr 1919	Torpedoed 20 Sept 1943
333	Q	*McCalla* (DD 253)	*Clemson* Class Destroyer	US Navy	New	19 May 1919	Torpedoed 19 Dec 1941
334	Q	*Rodgers* (DD 254)	*Clemson* Class Destroyer	US Navy	New	22 July 1919	Hulked 1943; Scrapped 1945
335	Q	*Osmond Ingram* (DD 255)	*Clemson* Class Destroyer	US Navy	New	27 June 1919	Scrapped 1946
336	Q	*Bancroft* (DD 256)	*Clemson* Class Destroyer	US Navy	New	30 June 1919	Collision 14 July 1945
337	Q	*Welles* (DD 257)	*Clemson* Class Destroyer	US Navy	New	2 Sept 1919	Bombed 5 Dec 1940: Scrapped 1944
338	Q	*Aulick* (DD 258)	*Clemson* Class Destroyer	US Navy	New	25 July 1919	Scrapped 1948
339	Q	*Turner* (DD 259)	*Clemson* Class Destroyer	US Navy	New	23 Sept 1919	Hulked 1936; Discarded 1946
340	Q	*Gillis* (DD 260)	*Clemson* Class Destroyer	US Navy	New	3 Sept 1919	Scrapped 1946
341	S	*Delphy* (DD 261)	*Clemson* Class Destroyer	US Navy	New	30 Nov 1918	Wrecked 8 Sept 1923
342	S	*McDermut* (DD 262)	*Clemson* Class Destroyer	US Navy	New	27 Mar 1919	Scrapped 1932
343	S	*Laub* (DD 263)	*Clemson* Class Destroyer	US Navy	New	17 Mar 1919	Scrapped 1947
344	S	*McLanahan* (DD 264)	*Clemson* Class Destroyer	US Navy	New	5 Apr 1919	Hulked 1943; Scrapped 1946
345	S	*Edwards* (DD 265)	*Clemson* Class Destroyer	US Navy	New	24 Apr 1919	Scrapped 1946
346	S	*Greene* (DD 266)	*Clemson* Class Destroyer	US Navy	New	9 May 1919	Wrecked 9 Oct 1945
347	S	*Ballard* (DD 267)	*Clemson* Class Destroyer	US Navy	New	5 June 1919	Scrapped 1946
348	S	*Shubrick* (DD 268)	*Clemson* Class Destroyer	US Navy	New	3 July 1919	Scrapped 1945
349	S	*Bailey* (DD 269)	*Clemson* Class Destroyer	US Navy	New	27 June 1919	Scrapped 1945
350	S	*Thornton* (DD 270)	*Clemson* Class Destroyer	US Navy	New	15 July 1919	Collision 5 Apr 1945; Abandoned
351	S	*Morris* (DD 271)	*Clemson* Class Destroyer	US Navy	New	21 July 1919	Scrapped 1936
352	S	*Tingey* (DD 272)	*Clemson* Class Destroyer	US Navy	New	25 July 1919	Scrapped 1936
		Swasey	*Clemson* Class			31 July	Mined 27 Sept

353	S	(DD 273)	Destroyer	US Navy	New	1919	1944
354	S	Meade (DD 274)	Clemson Class Destroyer	US Navy	New	8 Sept 1919	Scrapped 1947
355	S	Sinclair (DD 275)	Clemson Class Destroyer	US Navy	New	26 Aug 1919	Scrapped 1935
356	S	McCawley (DD 276)	Clemson Class Destroyer	US Navy	New	29 Aug 1919	Scrapped 1931
357	S	Moody (DD 277)	Clemson Class Destroyer	US Navy	New	26 Sept 1919	Scuttled 2/1933
358	S	Henshaw (DD 278)	Clemson Class Destroyer	US Navy	New	24 Sept 1919	Scrapped 1930
359	S	Meyer (DD 279)	Clemson Class Destroyer	US Navy	New	30 Sept 1919	Scrapped 1930
360	S	Doyen (DD 280)	Clemson Class Destroyer	US Navy	New	10 Oct 1919	Scrapped 1930
361	S	Sharkey (DD 281)	Clemson Class Destroyer	US Navy	New	20 Oct 1919	Scrapped 1931
362	S	Toucey (DD 282)	Clemson Class Destroyer	US Navy	New	31 Oct 1919	Scrapped 1934
363	S	Breck (DD 283)	Clemson Class Destroyer	US Navy	New	28 Nov 1919	Scrapped 1931
364	S	Isherwood (DD 284)	Clemson Class Destroyer	US Navy	New	26 Nov 1919	Scrapped 1934
365	S	Case (DD 285)	Clemson Class Destroyer	US Navy	New	29 Nov 1919	Scrapped 1931
366	S	Lardner (DD 286)	Clemson Class Destroyer	US Navy	New	10 Dec 1919	Scrapped 1931
367	S	Putnam (DD 287)	Clemson Class Destroyer	US Navy	New	18 Dec 1919	Scrapped 1931
368	S	Worden (DD 288)	Clemson Class Destroyer	US Navy	New	23 Dec 1919	Scrapped 1931
369	S	Flusser (DD 289)	Clemson Class Destroyer	US Navy	New	31 Dec 1919	Scrapped 1930
370	S	Dale (DD 290)	Clemson Class Destroyer	US Navy	New	14 Feb 1920	Scrapped 1931
371	S	Converse (DD 291)	Clemson Class Destroyer	US Navy	New	27 Apr 1920	Scrapped 1931
372	S	Reid (DD 292)	Clemson Class Destroyer	US Navy	New	6 Nov 1919	Scrapped 1931
373	S	Billingsley (DD 293)	Clemson Class Destroyer	US Navy	New	7 Feb 1920	Scrapped 1931
374	S	Charles Ausburn (DD 294)	Clemson Class Destroyer	US Navy	New	28 Feb 1920	Scrapped 1931
375	S	Osborne	Clemson Class	US Navy	New	17 May	Scrapped 1931

			(DD 295)	Destroyer				1920	
1376	Q		Watertown	432' Tanker	US Shipping Board	New		16 July 1919	Scrapped 1948
1377	Q		Baldbutte	432' Tanker	US Shipping Board	New		13 Aug 1919	Scrapped 1947
1378	Q		Baldhill	432' Tanker	US Shipping Board	New		20 Sept 1919	Scrapped 1948
1379	Q		Hadnot	432' Tanker	US Shipping Board	New		24 Oct 1919	Scrapped 1947
1380	Q		Hagan	432' Tanker	US Shipping Board	New		25 Nov 1919	Torpedoed 11 June 1942
1381	Q		Trimountain	432' Tanker	US Shipping Board	New		23 Dec 1919	Scrapped 1954
1382	Q		Raleigh (CL 7)	Omaha Class Light Cruiser	US Navy	New		6 Feb 1924	Scrapped 1946
1383	Q		Detroit (CL 8)	Omaha Class Light Cruiser	US Navy	New		31 July 1923	Scrapped 1947
1384	Q		Cubore	468' Ore Freighter	Ore Steamship Co.	New		2 Aug 1920	Unknown
1385	Q		China Arrow	485' Tanker	Standard Transp. Co.	New		1 Oct 1920	Torpedoed 5 Feb 1942
1386	Q		Japan Arrow	485' Tanker	Standard Transp. Co.	New		24 Nov 1920	Unknown
1387	Q		India Arrow	485' Tanker	Standard Transp. Co.	New		17 Mar 1921	Torpedoed 5 Feb 1942
1388	Q		Java Arrow	485' Tanker	Standard Transp. Co.	New		24 May 1921	Scrapped 1959
1389	Q		S-42 (SS 153)	S-42 Class Submarine	Electric Boat Corp. for US Navy	New		8 Aug 1923	Scrapped 1947
1390	Q		S-43 (SS 154)	S-42 Class Submarine	Electric Boat Corp. for US Navy	New		11 July 1923	Scrapped 1946
1391	Q		S-44 (SS 155)	S-42 Class Submarine	Electric Boat Corp. for US Navy	New		8 Jan 1924	Lost 7 Oct 1943
1392	Q		S-45 (SS 156)	S-42 Class Submarine	Electric Boat Corp. for US Navy	New		27 Sept 1923	Scrapped 1947
1393	Q		S-46 (SS 157)	S-42 Class Submarine	Electric Boat Corp. for US Navy	New		12 Nov 1923	Scrapped 1947
1394	Q		S-47 (SS 158)	S-42 Class Submarine	Electric Boat Corp. for US Navy	New		27 Feb 1924	Scrapped 1946
1395	Q		Agwibay	485' Tanker	Atlantic, Gulf &	New		23 June	Unknown

				West Indies Co.			1921	
1396	Q	J. Fletcher Farrell	446' Tanker	Sinclair Navigation Co.	New	6 June 1921	Unknown
1397	Q	Wm. Boyce Thompson	446' Tanker	Sinclair Navigation Co.	New	28 July 1921	Torpedoed 23 May 1942

Major Sources:
List of Ships Built at the Quincy Yard. Central Technical Department of Bethlehem Steel Company, Shipbuilding Division, Quincy, MA., with unofficial addenda.

Dictionary of American Naval Fighting Ships. Naval Historical Center, Washington, D.C., 1959-1991.

Special thanks to Michael Pryce for providing many ship fates, and to everyone who has provided updated information about these ships.

Back to the *Hazegray* Shipbuilding Pages

Fore River Shipyard Production Record

Part 2: Hull 1398 through Hull 1693
(1925 through 1963)

This is a complete list of all Fore River Shipyard production, listed in order by Fore River hull number. Small repair or overhaul jobs that were not assigned hull numbers are not included. During this period the yard was under the ownership of Bethlehem Steel.

This list was compiled and is maintained by Andrew Toppan, using sources listed at the bottom of the document.

The first column is the Fore River hull number, followed by the vessel's name, the type/size/class of the vessel, the owner/customer for the vessel, the type of work done (new construction, overhaul, etc.), the date the vessel was delivered, and the fate or status of the vessel. For ships that remain in existence the current name is listed in the status/fate column; if no name is listed, the vessel retains its original name.

For conversions and reconditionings, the vessel's new name (at completion) is listed under "name", the original name and description are listed under "type", and the nature of the conversion is listed under "work type".

Fore River Shipyard Production Record

Hull	Name	Type/Descr.	Owner	Work Type	Delivered	Fate or Status
1398	*Charles G. Donoghue*	174' Harbor Ferry	City of Boston	New	23 Sept 1926	Unknown
1399	*Daniel A. MacCormack*	174' Harbor Ferry	City of Boston	New	21 Oct 1926	Unknown
1400	*Massachusetts* (BB 54)	*South Dakota* Class Battleship	US Navy	New	--	Cancelled 17 Aug 1923
1401	*Governor Carr*	150' Harbor Ferry	Jamestown & Newport Co.	New	14 Feb 1927	Unknown
1402	*No. 65*	360' Carfloat	New York, New Haven & Hartford Ry	New	17 Jan 1927	Unknown
1403	*No. 66*	360' Carfloat	New York, New Haven & Hartford Ry	New	9 Feb 1927	Unknown

1404	No. 67	360' Carfloat	New York, New Haven & Hartford Ry	New	9 Apr 1927	Unknown
1405	No. 68	360' Carfloat	New York, New Haven & Hartford Ry	New	9 Apr 1927	Unknown
1406	*Unknown*					
1407	*Unknown*					
1408	Cities Service No. 2	212' Tank Barge	Cities Service Co.	New	20 Apr 1927	Unknown
1409	Cities Service No. 3	150' Tank Barge	Cities Service Co.	New	23 Aug 1927	Unknown
1410	Northampton (CL 26)	Northampton Class Light Cruiser	US Navy	New	15 May 1930	Torpedoed 30 Nov 1942
1411	Chelan (WPG 45)	Lake Class Cutter	US Coast Guard	New	20 Aug 1928	Discarded 1947
1412	Pontchartrain (WPG 46)	Lake Class Cutter	US Coast Guard	New	10 Oct 1928	Lost 8 Nov 1942
1413	Tahoe (WPG 47)	Lake Class Cutter	US Coast Guard	New	31 Oct 1928	Discarded 1947
1414	Champlain (WPG 48)	Lake Class Cutter	US Coast Guard	New	12 Jan 1929	Discarded 1948
1415	Mendota (WPG 49)	Lake Class Cutter	US Coast Guard	New	16 Mar 1929	Torpedoed 31 Jan 1942
1416	Edward F. Farrington	131' Coastal Freighter	Middlesex Transp. Co.	New	22 Feb 1928	Unknown
1417	New Bedford	210' Coastal Passenger Steamer	New England Steamship Co. (NY,NH&H Ry.)	New	19 May 1928	Abandoned 1968
1418	Virginia Lee	302' Passenger Steamer	Pennsylvania RR	New	25 Oct 1928	Scrapped 1968
1419	Shawmut	122' Trawler	Massachusetts Trawler Co.	New	5 Nov 1928	Unknown
1420	Trimount	122' Trawler	Massachusetts Trawler Co.	New	19 Nov 1928	Discarded 1946
1421	William J. O'Brien	122' Trawler	Massachusetts Trawler Co.	New	18 Dec 1928	Unknown
1422	Berwindglen	367' Collier	Wilmore Steamship Co.	New	23 July 1929	Barged 1950; Scrapped 1954
1423	Berwindvale	367' Collier	Wilmore Steamship Co.	New	21 Aug 1929	Scrapped 1952
1424	Naushon	250' Coastal Passenger / Freight Steamer	New England Steamship Co. (NY,NH&H Ry.)	New	20 May 1929	Scrapped 1974
1425	Seaboard No. 1	165' Tank Barge	Seaboard Shipping Corp.	New	19 June 1929	Unknown
1426	No-Nox	209' Tank Barge	Gulf Refining Co.	New	20 Aug 1929	Unknown

Fore River Shipyard Production Record, Part 2

1427	Quincy	110' Trawler	R. O'Brien & Co.	New	18 Dec 1929	Unknown
1428	Dorchester	110' Trawler	R. O'Brien & Co.	New	6 Jan 1930	Unknown
1429	Winthrop	110' Trawler	R. O'Brien & Co.	New	26 Dec 1929	Unknown
1430	Portland (CA 33)	Portland Class Heavy Cruiser	US Navy	New	15 Feb 1933	Scrapped 1969
1431	Cities Service No. 4	200' Tank Barge	Cities Service Co.	New	20 Nov 1929	Unknown
1432	Borinquen	429' Freighter	New York & Porto Rico Co.	New	20 Feb 1931	Wrecked 13 Apr 1970
1433	Dartmouth	110' Trawler	General Seafoods Corp.	New	27 Jan 1930	Unknown
1434	Amherst	110' Trawler	General Seafoods Corp.	New	7 Feb 1930	Unknown
1435	Cornell	110' Trawler	General Seafoods Corp.	New	15 Feb 1930	Unknown
1436	L.T.C. No. 1	201' Tank Barge	Lake Tankers Corp.	New	30 May 1930	Unknown
1437	L.T.C. No. 2	201' Tank Barge	Lake Tankers Corp.	New	13 June 1930	Unknown
1438	Virginia Sinclair	435' Tanker	Sinclair Navigation Co.	New	20 Dec 1930	Torpedoed 10 Mar 1943
1439	Harry F. Sinclair Jr.	435' Tanker	Sinclair Navigation Co.	New	28 Feb 1931	Torpedoed 11 Apr 1942
1440	Mariposa	631' Passenger Liner	Oceanic Steamship Co.	New	14 Dec 1931	Scrapped 1974
1441	Monterey	631' Passenger Liner	Oceanic Steamship Co.	New	29 Apr 1932	Laid Up (Belofin I)
1442	L.T.C. No. 3	201' Tank Barge	Lake Tankers Corp.	New	1 July 1930	Unknown
1443	General Sumner	174' Harbor Ferry	City of Boston	New	6 Jan 1931	Unknown
1444	Antigua	447' Freighter	United Mail Steamship Co.	New	1 Apr 1932	Scrapped 1964
1445	Quirigua	447' Freighter	United Mail Steamship Co.	New	4 June 1932	Scrapped 1964
1446	Veragua	447' Freighter	United Mail Steamship Co.	New	5 Aug 1932	Scrapped 1964
1447	Lurline	631' Passenger Liner	Oceanic Steamship Co.	New	5 Jan 1933	Scrapped 1987
1448	Farragut (DD 348)	Farragut Class Destroyer	US Navy	New	18 June 1934	Scrapped 1947
1449	Vincennes (CA 44)	New Orleans Class Heavy Cruiser	US Navy	New	24 Feb 1937	Torpedoed 9 Aug 1942
1450	Quincy (CA 39)	New Orleans Class Heavy Cruiser	US Navy	New	9 June 1936	Torpedoed 9 Aug 1942

1451	Phelps (DD 360)	Porter Class Destroyer Leader	US Navy	New	26 Feb 1936	Scrapped 1947
1452	Clark (DD 361)	Porter Class Destroyer Leader	US Navy	New	20 May 1936	Scrapped 1946
1453	Moffett (DD 362)	Porter Class Destroyer Leader	US Navy	New	28 Aug 1936	Scrapped 1947
1454	Balch (DD 363)	Porter Class Destroyer Leader	US Navy	New	20 Oct 1936	Scrapped 1946
1455	Thomas Whalen	110' Trawler	R. O'Brien & Co.	New	9 Oct 1934	Unknown
1456	Atlantic	110' Trawler	R. O'Brien & Co.	New	25 Oct 1934	Unknown
1457	Plymouth	110' Trawler	R. O'Brien & Co.	New	29 Oct 1934	Unknown
1458	Gridley (DD 380)	Gridley Class Destroyer	US Navy	New	24 June 1937	Scrapped 1947
1459	Craven (DD 382)	Gridley Class Destroyer	US Navy	New	2 Sept 1937	Scrapped 1947
1460	Wasp (CV 7)	Wasp Class Aircraft Carrier	US Navy	New	25 Apr 1940	Torpedoed 15 Sept 1942
1461	Neptune	110' Trawler	Neptune Trawling Co.	New	1 Sept 1936	Unknown
1462	Triton	110' Trawler	Triton Trawling Co.	New	16 Sept 1936	Unknown
1463	Goethals	476' Hopper Dredge	US Army Corps of Engineers	New	28 Dec 1937	Unknown
1464	Annapolis	147' Trawler	General Seafoods	New	19 Oct 1937	Unknown
1465	West Point	147' Trawler	General Seafoods	New	29 Oct 1937	Unknown
1466	Yale	147' Trawler	General Seafoods	New	26 Nov 1937	Unknown
1467	Panama	493' Freighter	Panama RR Co.	New	21 Apr 1939	Scrapped 1985
1468	Ancon	493' Freighter	Panama RR Co.	New	16 June 1939	Scrapped 1973
1469	Cristobal	493' Freighter	Panama RR Co.	New	11 Aug 1939	Scrapped 1981
1470	Benson (DD 421)	Benson Class Destroyer	US Navy	New	25 July 1940	Discarded 1975
1471	Mayo (DD 422)	Benson Class Destroyer	US Navy	New	18 Sept 1940	Discarded 1970
1472	Wave	147' Trawler	General Seafoods	New	18 Nov 1938	Discarded 1945
1473	Crest	147' Trawler	General Seafoods	New	20 Dec 1938	Unknown

1474	*Exporter*	473' C3 Freighter	American Export Lines	New	28 Sept 1939	Scrapped 1971
1475	*Explorer*	473' C3 Freighter	American Export Lines	New	16 Nov 1939	Scrapped 1970
1476	*Exchange*	473' C3 Freighter	American Export Lines	New	23 Feb 1940	Unknown
1477	*Express*	473' C3 Freighter	American Export Lines	New	18 Apr 1940	Unknown
1478	*Massachusetts* (BB 59)	*South Dakota* Class Battleship	US Navy	New	12 May 1942	Preserved @ Fall River
1479	*San Diego* (CL 53)	*Atlanta* Class Antiaircraft Cruiser	US Navy	New	10 Jan 1942	Scrapped 1960
1480	*San Juan* (CL 54)	*Atlanta* Class Antiaircraft Cruiser	US Navy	New	28 Feb 1942	Scrapped 1962
1481	*Exemplar*	473' C3 Freighter	American Export Lines	New	1 Aug 1940	Unknown (USS *Dorothea L. Dix* (AP 67))
1482	*Exhibitor*	473' C3 Freighter	American Export Lines	New	5 Sept 1940	Unknown
1483	*Executor*	473' C3 Freighter	American Export Lines	New	22 Oct 1940	Unknown (USS *Almaack* (AKA 10))
1484	*Examiner*	473' C3 Freighter	American Export Lines	New	23 Jan 1942	Unknown
1485	*Stanvac Calcutta*	501' Tanker	Petroluem Shipping Co. (Standard Vacuum Co.)	New	1 May 1941	Sunk 6 June 1942
1486	*Stanvac Capetown*	501' Tanker	Petroluem Shipping Co. (Standard Vacuum Co.)	New	27 June 1941	Scrapped 1960
1487	*Stanvac Manila*	501' Tanker	Petroluem Shipping Co. (Standard Vacuum Co.)	New	1 Aug 1941	Torpedoed 23 May 1943
1488	*Sinclair Opaline*	471' Tanker	Sinclair Refining Co.	New	16 Aug 1941	Scrapped 1961
1489	*Sinclair Rubilene*	471' Tanker	Sinclair Refining Co.	New	20 Sept 1941	Scrapped 1959
1490	*Sinclair Superflame*	471' Tanker	Sinclair Refining Co.	New	7 Nov 1941	Scrapped 1966
1491	*Sinclair H-C*	471' Tanker	Sinclair Refining Co.	New	6 Jan 1942	Discarded 1980's
1492	*Flagship Sinco*	529' Tanker	Sinclair Refining Co.	New	30 Jan 1942	Scrapped 1970
1493	*Sheldon Clark*	529' Tanker	Sinclair Refining Co.	New	28 Mar 1942	Scrapped 1973
1494	*Baltimore* (CA 68)	*Baltimore* Class Heavy Cruiser	US Navy	New	15 Apr 1943	Discarded 1971

162   THE SHIPYARD

1495	Boston (CA 69)	Baltimore Class Heavy Cruiser	US Navy	New	30 June 1943	Scrapped 1975
1496	Canberra (CA 70)	Baltimore Class Heavy Cruiser	US Navy	New	14 Oct 1943	Scrapped 1980
1497	Quincy (CA 71)	Baltimore Class Heavy Cruiser	US Navy	New	15 Dec 1943	Discarded 1973
1498	Vincennes (CL 64)	Cleveland Class Light Cruiser	US Navy	New	21 Jan 1944	Target 28 Oct 1969
1499	Pasadena (CL 65)	Cleveland Class Light Cruiser	US Navy	New	8 June 1944	Discarded 1970
1500	Springfield (CL 66)	Cleveland Class Light Cruiser	US Navy	New	8 Sept 1944	Discarded 1978
1501	Topeka (CL 67)	Cleveland Class Light Cruiser	US Navy	New	23 Dec 1944	Scrapped 1975
1502	Providence (CL 82)	Cleveland Class Light Cruiser	US Navy	New	14 May 1945	Discarded 1978
1503	Mancester (CL 83)	Cleveland Class Light Cruiser	US Navy	New	25 Oct 1946	Scrapped 1960
1504	Pittsburgh (CA 72)	Baltimore Class Heavy Cruiser	US Navy	New	9 Oct 1944	Discarded 1973
1505	Saint Paul (CA 73)	Baltimore Class Heavy Cruiser	US Navy	New	16 Feb 1945	Discarded 1978
1506	Columbus (CA 74)	Baltimore Class Heavy Cruiser	US Navy	New	8 June 1945	Discarded 1976
1507	Helena (CA 75)	Baltimore Class Heavy Cruiser	US Navy	New	3 Sept 1945	Discarded 1974
1508	Lexington (CV 16)	Essex Class Aircraft Carrier	US Navy	New	17 Feb 1943	Preserved @ Corpus Christi
1509	Bunker Hill (CV 17)	Essex Class Aircraft Carrier	US Navy	New	24 May 1943	Scrapped 1974
1510	Wasp (CV 18)	Essex Class Aircraft Carrier	US Navy	New	24 Nov 1943	Scrapped 1973
1511	Hancock (CV 19)	Essex Class Aircraft Carrier	US Navy	New	15 Apr 1944	Discarded 1976
1512	Cohasset	110' Trawler	R. O'Brien & Co.	New	9 Oct 1941	Unknown
1513	Lynn	110' Trawler	R. O'Brien & Co.	New	22 Oct 1941	Unknown
1514	Salem	110' Trawler	R. O'Brien & Co.	New	6 Nov 1941	Unknown
1515	Weymouth	110' Trawler	R. O'Brien & Co.	New	26 Nov 1941	Unknown
1516	Bancroft (DD 598)	Benson Class Destroyer	US Navy	New	30 Apr 1942	Discarded 1971
1517	Barton (DD 599)	Benson Class Destroyer	US Navy	New	29 May 1942	Torpedoed 13 Nov 1942
1518	Boyle	Benson Class	US Navy	New	15 Aug	Discarded 1971

					1942	
	(DD 600)	Destroyer			1942	
1519	*Champlin* (DD 601)	*Benson* Class Destroyer	US Navy	New	12 Sept 1942	Discarded 1971
1520	*Nields* (DD 616)	*Benson* Class Destroyer	US Navy	New	15 Jan 1943	Discarded 1971
1521	*Ordronaux* (DD 617)	*Benson* Class Destroyer	US Navy	New	13 Feb 1943	Discarded 1971
1522	*LST 361*	LST *1* Class Tank Landing Ship	US Navy for Royal Navy	New	16 Nov 1942	Scrapped 1947
1523	*LST 362*	LST *1* Class Tank Landing Ship	US Navy for Royal Navy	New	23 Nov 1942	Torpedoed 2 March 1944
1524	*LST 363*	LST *1* Class Tank Landing Ship	US Navy for Royal Navy	New	30 Nov 1942	Scrapped 1948
1525	*LST 364*	LST *i* Class Tank Landing Ship	US Navy for Royal Navy	New	7 Dec 1942	Lost 2/1945
1526	*LST 365*	LST *1* Class Tank Landing Ship	US Navy for Royal Navy	New	14 Dec 1942	Discarded 1947
1527	*LST 366*	LST *1* Class Tank Landing Ship	US Navy for Royal Navy	New	21 Dec 1942	Scrapped 1947
1528	*LST 367*	LST *1* Class Tank Landing Ship	US Navy for Royal Navy	New	29 Dec 1942	Scrapped 1948
1529	*LST 368*	LST *1* Class Tank Landing Ship	US Navy for Royal Navy	New	4 Jan 1943	Destroyed 16 June 1948
1530	*LST 369*	LST *1* Class Tank Landing Ship	US Navy	New	8 Jan 1943	Discarded 1947
1531	*LST 370*	LST *1* Class Tank Landing Ship	US Navy	New	13 Jan 1943	Discarded 1947
1532	*LST 371*	LST *1* Class Tank Landing Ship	US Navy	New	16 Jan 1943	Discarded 1947
1533	*LST 372*	LST *1* Class Tank Landing Ship	US Navy	New	23 Jan 1943	Scrapped 1947
1534	*LST 373*	LST *1* Class Tank Landing Ship	US Navy	New	27 Jan 1943	Discarded 1947
1535	*LST 374*	LST *1* Class Tank Landing Ship	US Navy	New	29 Jan 1943	Discarded 1947
1536	*LST 375*	LST *1* Class Tank Landing Ship	US Navy	New	2 Feb 1943	Scrapped 1949
1537	*LST 376*	LST *1* Class Tank Landing Ship	US Navy	New	5 Feb 1943	Torpedoed 9 June 1944
1538	*LST 377*	LST *1* Class Tank Landing Ship	US Navy	New	8 Feb 1943	Scrapped 1948
1539	*LST 378*	LST *1* Class Tank Landing Ship	US Navy	New	10 Feb 1943	Discarded 1947
1540	*LST 379*	LST *1* Class Tank Landing Ship	US Navy	New	12 Feb 1943	Scrapped 1948

1541	LST 380	LST 1 Class Tank Landing Ship	US Navy	New	15 Feb 1943	Discarded 1946
1542	LST 381	LST 1 Class Tank Landing Ship	US Navy	New	15 Feb 1943	Scrapped 1947
1543	LST 382	LST 1 Class Tank Landing Ship	US Navy	New	18 Feb 1943	Discarded 1948
1544	Oregon City (CA 122)	Oregon City Class Heavy Cruiser	US Navy	New	15 Feb 1946	Discarded 1970
1545	Albany (CA 123)	Oregon City Class Heavy Cruiser	US Navy	New	14 June 1946	Scrapped 1990
1546	Rochester (CA 124)	Oregon City Class Heavy Cruiser	US Navy	New	19 Dec 1946	Discarded 1973
1547	Northampton (CA 125)	Oregon City Class Heavy Cruiser	US Navy	New	--	Cancelled 13 Aug 1945; Discarded 1977
1548	Cambridge (CA 126)	Oregon City Class Heavy Cruiser	US Navy	New	--	Cancelled 13 Aug 1945
1549	Bridgeport (CA 127)	Oregon City Class Heavy Cruiser	US Navy	New	--	Cancelled 13 Aug 1945
1550	Kansas City (CA 128)	Oregon City Class Heavy Cruiser	US Navy	New	--	Cancelled 13 Aug 1945
1551	Tulsa (CA 129)	Oregon City Class Heavy Cruiser	US Navy	New	--	Cancelled 13 Aug 1945
1552	Weber (DE 675)	Buckley (TE) Class Destroyer Escort	US Navy	New	30 June 1943	Target 15 July 1962
1553	Schmitt (DE 676)	Buckley (TE) Class Destroyer Escort	US Navy	New	24 July 1943	Discarded 1976
1554	Frament (DE 677)	Buckley (TE) Class Destroyer Escort	US Navy	New	15 Aug 1943	Discarded 1960
1555	Harmon (DE 678)	Buckley (TE) Class Destroyer Escort	US Navy	New	31 Aug 1943	Scrapped 1967
1556	Greenwood (DE 679)	Buckley (TE) Class Destroyer Escort	US Navy	New	25 Sept 1943	Scrapped 1967
1557	Loeser (DE 680)	Buckley (TE) Class Destroyer Escort	US Navy	New	10 Oct 1943	Target 1960's
1558	Gillette (DE 681)	Buckley (TE) Class Destroyer Escort	US Navy	New	27 Oct 1943	Scrapped 1973
1559	Underhill (DE 682)	Buckley (TE) Class Destroyer Escort	US Navy	New	15 Nov 1943	Torpedoed 24 July 1945
1560	Henry R. Kenyon (DE 683)	Buckley (TE) Class Destroyer Escort	US Navy	New	30 Nov 1943	Scrapped 1970
1561	DeLong (DE 684)	Buckley (TE) Class Destroyer Escort	US Navy	New	31 Dec 1943	Target 19 Feb 1970
1562	Coates (DE 685)	Buckley (TE) Class Destroyer Escort	US Navy	New	24 Jan 1944	Target 19 Sept 1971

1563	Eugene E. Elmore (DE 686)	Buckley (TE) Class Destroyer Escort	US Navy	New	4 Feb 1944	Scrapped 1969
1564	Kline (APD 120)	Crosley Class High Speed Transport	US Navy	New	18 Oct 1944	In Service (Taiwanese Shou Shan)
1565	Raymon W. Herndon (APD 121)	Crosley Class High Speed Transport	US Navy	New	3 Nov 1944	Discarded 1976
1566	Scribner (APD 122)	Crosley Class High Speed Transport	US Navy	New	20 Nov 1944	Scrapped 1967
1567	Alex Diachenko (APD 123)	Crosley Class High Speed Transport	US Navy	New	8 Dec 1944	Scrapped 1975
1568	Horace A. Bass (APD 124)	Crosley Class High Speed Transport	US Navy	New	21 Dec 1944	Scrapped 1975
1569	Wantuck (APD 125)	Crosley Class High Speed Transport	US Navy	New	30 Dec 1944	Scrapped 1958
1570	Philippine Sea (CV 47)	Essex Class Aircraft Carrier	US Navy	New	3 May 1946	Scrapped 1971
1571	Des Moines (CA 134)	Salem Class Heavy Cruiser	US Navy	New	15 Nov 1948	Stricken 1991; Pending Disposal
1572	Salem (CA 139)	Salem Class Heavy Cruiser	US Navy	New	9 May 1949	Preserved @ Quincy
1573	Dallas (CA 140)	Salem Class Heavy Cruiser	US Navy	New	--	Cancelled 10 June 1946
1574	CA 141	Salem Class Heavy Cruiser	US Navy	New	--	Cancelled 7 Jan 1946
1575	CA 142	Salem Class Heavy Cruiser	US Navy	New	--	Cancelled 13 Aug 1945
1576	Joseph P. Kennedy Jr. (DD 850)	Gearing Class Destroyer	US Navy	New	14 Dec 1945	Preserved @ Fall River
1577	Rupertus (DD 851)	Gearing Class Destroyer	US Navy	New	8 Mar 1946	Discarded 1995
1578	Leonard F. Mason (DD 852)	Gearing Class Destroyer	US Navy	New	28 June 1946	In Service (Taiwanese Sui Yang)
1579	Charles H. Roan (DD 853)	Gearing Class Destroyer	US Navy	New	12 Sept 1946	Scrapped 1995
1580	LST 1004	LST 511 Class Tank Landing Ship	US Navy	New	28 Mar 1944	Scrapped 1947
1581	LST 1005	LST 511 Class Tank Landing Ship	US Navy	New	6 Apr 1944	Wrecked 1946
1582	LST 1006	LST 511 Class Tank Landing Ship	US Navy	New	12 Apr 1944	Discarded 1948

166   THE SHIPYARD

1583	LST 1007	LST 511 Class Tank Landing Ship	US Navy	New	15 Apr 1944	Discarded 1946
1584	LST 1008	LST 511 Class Tank Landing Ship	US Navy	New	18 Apr 1944	Discarded 1946
1585	LST 1009	LST 511 Class Tank Landing Ship	US Navy	New	22 Apr 1944	Discarded 1946
1586	LST 1010	LST 511 Class Tank Landing Ship	US Navy	New	25 Apr 1944	In Service (South Korean *Un Bong*)
1587	LST 1011	LST 511 Class Tank Landing Ship	US Navy	New	28 Apr 1944	Scrapped 1948
1588	LST 1012	LST 511 Class Tank Landing Ship	US Navy	New	30 Apr 1944	Discarded 1946
1589	LST 1013	LST 511 Class Tank Landing Ship	US Navy	New	2 May 1944	Discarded 1946
1590	LST 1014	LST 511 Class Tank Landing Ship	US Navy	New	5 May 1944	Discarded 1946
1591	LST 1015	LST 511 Class Tank Landing Ship	US Navy	New	7 May 1944	Discarded 1946
1592	LST 1016	LST 511 Class Tank Landing Ship	US Navy	New	10 May 1944	Scrapped 1948
1593	LST 1017	LST 511 Class Tank Landing Ship	US Navy	New	12 May 1944	Discarded 1946
1594	LST 1018	LST 511 Class Tank Landing Ship	US Navy	New	14 May 1944	Scrapped 1948
1595	LST 1019	LST 511 Class Tank Landing Ship	US Navy	New	17 May 1944	Discarded 1948
1596	LST 1020	LST 511 Class Tank Landing Ship	US Navy	New	19 May 1944	Scrapped 1948
1597	LST 1021	LST 511 Class Tank Landing Ship	US Navy	New	24 May 1944	Discarded 1947
1598	LST 1022	LST 511 Class Tank Landing Ship	US Navy	New	24 May 1944	Scrapped 1948
1599	LST 1023	LST 511 Class Tank Landing Ship	US Navy	New	26 May 1944	Discarded 1948
1600	LST 1024	LST 511 Class Tank Landing Ship	US Navy	New	28 May 1944	Discarded 1948
1601	LST 1025	LST 511 Class Tank Landing Ship	US Navy	New	31 May 1944	Discarded 1948
1602	LST 1026	LST 511 Class Tank Landing Ship	US Navy	New	7 June 1944	Discarded 1947
1603	LST 1027	LST 511 Class Tank Landing Ship	US Navy	New	7 June 1944	Discarded 1947
1604	CA 143	*Salem* Class Heavy Cruiser	US Navy	New	--	Cancelled 13 Aug 1945
		Essex Class				Cancelled 27

Fore River Shipyard Production Record, Part 2

1605	CV 50	Aircraft Carrier	US Navy	New	--	Mar 1945
1606	*Basilone* (DDE 824)	*Gearing* Class Destroyer (Incomplete)	US Navy	Completion as *Epperson* Class Escort Destroyer	21 July 1949	Discarded 1977
1607	*Pennsylvania*	28,000 DWT, 624' Tanker	Texas Co. (Texaco)	New	5 Aug 1949	Scrapped 1985
1608	*Texas*	28,000 DWT, 624' Tanker	Texas Co. (Texaco)	New	31 Aug 1949	Scrapped 1986
1609	*Ohio*	28,000 DWT, 624' Tanker	Texas Co. (Texaco)	New	21 Oct 1949	Scrapped 1985
1610	*Kentucky*	28,000 DWT, 624' Tanker	Texas Co. (Texaco)	New	26 Oct 1949	Scrapped 1985
1611	*World Liberty*	28,000 DWT, 624' Tanker	World Tankers Co. (Niarchos)	New	30 Nov 1949	Collision 12 March 1966; Scrapped
1612	*Northampton* (CLC 1)	*Oregon City* Class Heavy Cruiser (Incomplete)	US Navy	Completion as *Northampton* Class Tactical Command Ship	28 Feb 1953	Discarded 1977
1613	*Capsa*	28,000 DWT, 624' Tanker	Atlas Tankers, Inc.	New	11 Jan 1950	Scrapped 1976
1614	*Capulus*	28,000 DWT, 624' Tanker	Atlas Tankers, Inc.	New	15 Mar 1950	Scrapped 1975
1615	*Caperata*	28,000 DWT, 624' Tanker	Atlas Tankers, Inc.	New	12 Apr 1950	Scrapped 1976
1616	*Caprella*	28,000 DWT, 624' Tanker	Atlas Tankers, Inc.	New	14 June 1950	Scrapped 1977
1617	*Caprinus*	28,000 DWT, 624' Tanker	Atlas Tankers, Inc.	New	14 Sept 1950	Scrapped 1978
1618	*Independence*	682' Passenger Liner	American Export Lines	New	11 Jan 1951	In Service
1619	*Constitution*	682' Passenger Liner	American Export Lines	New	7 June 1951	Lost 24 Nov 1997
1620	*Willis A. Lee* (DL 4)	*Mitscher* Class Frigate	US Navy	New	29 Sept 1954	Scrapped 1973
1621	*Wilkinson* (DL 5)	*Mitscher* Class Frigate	US Navy	New	29 July 1954	Scrapped 1975
1622	*Old Colony Mariner*	*Mariner* Class 563' C4-S-1a Freighter	US Maritime Administration	New	28 Oct 1952	Scrapped 1980
1623	*Cornhusker Mariner*	*Mariner* Class 563' C4-S-1a Freighter	US Maritime Administration	New	5 Jan 1953	Wrecked 7 July 1953; Scrapped
1624	*Pine Tree Mariner*	*Mariner* Class 563' C4-S-1a Freighter	US Maritime Administration	New	3 Apr 1953	Unknown (*Mariposa*)
1625	*Nutmeg Mariner*	*Mariner* Class 563' C4-S-1a Freighter	US Maritime Administration	New	9 Sept 1953	Wrecked 8 oct 1961
1626	*Wolverine*	*Mariner* Class 563'	US Maritime	New	30 Oct	Unknown

http://www.hazegray.org/shipbuilding/quincy/fore2.htm

2/22/03

	Mariner	C4-S-1a Freighter	Administration		1953	(Arizona)
1627	Failaika	28,000 DWT, 624' Tanker	Afran Transport Co. (Gulf)	New	3 July 1952	Scrapped 1980
1628	La Cruz	28,000 DWT, 624' Tanker	Afran Transport Co. (Gulf)	New	18 Sept 1952	Scrapped 1980
1629	Waneta	29,000 DWT, 644' Tanker	Brilliant Transport Co. (Socony-Vacuum Oil Co.)	New	11 Dec 1952	Scrapped 1977
1630	Chryssi	29,000 DWT, 644' Tanker	Santander Compania Naviera, S.A. (Orion)	New	26 Feb 1953	Sunk 26 Dec 1970
1631	Andros Island	29,000 DWT, 644' Tanker	Rio Venturado Compania Naviera, S.A. (Orion)	New	7 May 1953	Scrapped 1975
1632	Andros Hills	29,000 DWT, 644' Tanker	Rio Venturado Compania Naviera, S.A. (Orion)	New	12 Aug 1953	Scrapped 1972
1633	Neosho (AO 143)	Neosho Class Fleet Oiler	US Navy	New	17 Sept 1954	Stricken 1994
1634	Orion Comet	29,000 DWT, 644' Tanker	Oil Carriers Joint Venture (Orion)	New	16 Oct 1953	Lost 12/1976
1635	Master Peter	29,000 DWT, 644' Tanker	Bilbao Compania Naviera, S.A. (Orion)	New	8 Oct 1954	Scrapped 1977
1636	George Livanos	29,000 DWT, 644' Tanker	Atlantic Oil Carriers Ltd. (Livanos)	New	11 Jan 1954	Scrapped 1976
1637	Athina Livanos	29,000 DWT, 644' Tanker	Atlantic Oil Carriers Ltd. (Livanos)	New	9 Sept 1954	Scrapped 1977
1638	Marine Dow-Chem	16,600 DWT, 551' Chemical Tanker	Marine Chemicals Transport Co.	New	26 Mar 1954	Barged 1974
1639	World Glory	45,500 DWT, 736' Tanker	World Tankers Co. (Niarchos)	New	19 Aug 1954	Sunk 14 June 1968
1640	Unknown					
1641	Unknown					
1642	Contract Transferred to Bethlehem Sparrows Point					
1643	Margarita	29,000 DWT, 644' Tanker	Afran Transport Co. (Gulf)	New	15 July 1954	Scrapped 1979
1644	--	29,000 DWT, 644' Tanker	Reconquista Compania Panamena de Naviera (Konialidis)	New	--	Cancelled
1645	Unknown					
1646	Unknown					
1647	Socony-Vacuum	27,000 DWT, 604' Tanker	Socony- Vacuum Oil Co.	New	3 Dec 1954	Scrapped 1985
1648	Decatur (DD 936)	Forrest Sherman Class Destroyer	US Navy	New	30 Nov 1956	In Service (ex-Decatur)

1649	Davis (DD 937)	Forrest Sherman Class Destroyer	US Navy	New	28 Feb 1957	Scrapped 1996
1650	Jonas Ingram (DD 938)	Forrest Sherman Class Destroyer	US Navy	New	10 July 1957	Target 20 July 1988
1651	Blandy (DD 943)	Forrest Sherman Class Destroyer	US Navy	New	20 Nov 1957	Scrapped 1996
1652	Mullinix (DD 944)	Forrest Sherman Class Destroyer	US Navy	New	26 Feb 1958	Target 22 Aug 1992
1653	--	Offshore Radar Platform - Georges Bank Station	US Navy / US Air Force	New	13 June 1955	Demolished 1963-1964
1654	Mobilgas	27,000 DWT, 604' Tanker	Charles Kurz & Co.	New	17 May 1956	Scrapped 1984
1655	World Beauty	45,500 DWT, 736' Tanker	World Beauty Corp. (Niarchos)	New	18 Apr 1957	Scrapped 1977
1656	Farragut (DLG 6)	Farragut Class Frigate	US Navy	New	8 Dec 1960	Stricken 1992
1657	Luce (DLG 7)	Farragut Class Frigate	US Navy	New	11 May 1961	Stricken 1992
1658	Macdonough (DLG 8)	Farragut Class Frigate	US Navy	New	29 Oct 1961	Stricken 1992
1659	Mobil Fuel	29,000 DWT, 644' Tanker	Kurz Tankers	New	Unknown	Laid Up (Meacham)
1660	Mobil Power	29,000 DWT, 644' Tanker	Kurz Tankers	New	27 Sept 1957	Laid Up (Naeco)
1661	Olympic Eagle	46,000 DWT, 736' Tanker	Greenwich Panama, S.A. (Onassis)	New	27 Aug 1958	Scrapped 1979
1662	Olympic Falcon	46,000 DWT, 736' Tanker	Occidental Shipping Co., S.A. (Onassis)	New	8 Dec 1958	Scrapped 1979
1663	Mobil Lube	29,000 DWT, 644' Tanker	Socony Mobil Oil Co.	New	10 Jan 1958	Scrapped 1983
1664	--	46,000 DWT, 736' Tanker	Bahama Marine S.A. (Onassis)	New	--	Cancelled 25 Nov 1957
1665	Princes Sophie	71,000 DWT, 859' Tanker	World Brilliance Corp. (Niarchos)	New	18 Mar 1959	Scrapped 1977
1666	Subcontracted to Bethlehem Sparrows Point					
1667	Subcontracted to Bethlehem Sparrows Point					
1668	Transeastern	46,000 DWT, 736' Tanker	Transeastern Shipping Corp.	New	30 July 1959	Scrapped 1995
1669	Long Beach (CGN 9)	Long Beach Class Guided Missile Cruiser	US Navy	New	1 Sept 1961	Stricken 1995; Pending Scrapping
1670	--	106,000 DWT, 940' Tanker	Goldensea Panama, S.A. (Onassis)	New	--	Cancelled 25 Nov 1957
1671	Mount Vernon Victory	46,000 DWT, 736' Tanker	Mount Vernon Tanker Co. (Onassis)	New	27 Jan 1961	Laid Up (Mount Vernon)

1672	Monticello Victory	46,000 DWT, 736' Tanker	Monticello Tanker Co. (Onassis)	New	Unk.	Burned 31 May 1981; Scrapped 1984
1673	Patro	46,000 DWT, 736' Tanker	Hercules Tankers Corp./Tanker Owners, S.A.	New	20 Feb 1959	Scrapped 1979
1674	Capulonix	46,000 DWT, 736' Tanker	Hercules Tankers Corp./Asiatic Petroleum Corp.	New	25 Sept 1959	Scrapped 1979
1675	Capiluna	46,000 DWT, 736' Tanker	Hercules Tankers Corp./Asiatic Petroleum Corp.	New	21 Oct 1960	Scrapped 1980
1676	Leland I. Doan	16,500 DWT, 551' Chemical Tanker	Chemical Tanker Marine Interests Corp.	New	3 Feb 1961	Scrapped 1985
1677	Bainbridge (DLGN 25)	Bainbridge Class Frigate	US Navy	New	28 Aug 1962	Stricken 1995; Pending Scrapping
1678			*Subcontracted to Bethlehem Sparrows Point*			
1679	Manhattan	106,500 DWT, 940' Tanker	Manhattan Tankers Co. (Niarchos)	New	15 Jan 1962	Scrapped 1987
1680	Orion Hunter	67,000 DWT, 860' Tanker	Colonial Tankers Corp. (Orion)	New	20 Dec 1961	Scrapped 1989
1681	--	106,500 DWT, 940' Tanker	1681 Corp./ Victory Carriers (Onassis)	New	--	Cancelled 9 June 1961
1682			*Subcontracted to Bethlehem Sparrows Point*			
1683			*Subcontracted to Bethlehem Sparrows Point*			
1684	American Courier	560' C4-S-57a Freighter	United States Lines	New	8 Feb 1963	Scrapped 1986
1685	American Commander	560' C4-S-57a Freighter	United States Lines	New	17 Apr 1963	Laid Up (Pioneer Commander)
1686	American Corsair	560' C4-S-57a Freighter	United States Lines	New	7 June 1963	Scrapped 1686
1687	American Contractor	560' C4-S-57a Freighter	United States Lines	New	Unk.	Laid Up (Pioneer Contractor)
1688	American Contender	560' C4-S-57a Freighter	United States Lines	New	Unk.	Unknown
1689	American Crusader	560' C4-S-57a Freighter	United States Lines	New	Unk.	Laid Up (Pioneer Crusader)
1690	Montpelier Victory	47,000 DWT, 736' Tanker	1681 Corp./ Victory Carriers (Onassis)	New	25 Oct 1962	Scrapped 1985
1691	Mount Washington	47,000 DWT, 736' Tanker	1681 Corp./ Victory Carriers (Onassis)	New	31 Oct 1963	In Reserve
1692	Whale (SSN 638)	Sturgeon Class Attack Submarine	Built by General Dynamics / Quincy Shipbuilding Division			
1693	Sunfish	Sturgeon Class	Built by General Dynamics / Quincy Shipbuilding Division			

| (SSN 649) | Attack Submarine |

Major Sources:
List of Ships Built at the Quincy Yard. Central Technical Department of Bethlehem Steel Company, Shipbuilding Division, Quincy, MA., with unofficial addenda.

Dictionary of American Naval Fighting Ships. Naval Historical Center, Washington, D.C., 1959-1991.

Special thanks to Michael Pryce for providing many ship fates, and to everyone who has provided updated information about these ships.

Back to the *Hazegray* Shipbuilding Pages

Fore River Shipyard Production Record, Part 3

Fore River Shipyard Production Record

Part 3: General Dynamics Quincy Shipbuilding Division (1963 through 1986)

This is a complete list of all Fore River Shipyard production, listed in order by hull number. Small repair or overhaul jobs that were not assigned hull numbers are not included. During this period the yard was under General Dynamics ownership and was known as the Quincy Shipbuilding Division of General Dynamics.

This list was compiled and is maintained by Andrew Toppan, using sources listed at the bottom of the document.

The first column is the Electric Boat or Quincy hull number (when known), followed by the vessel's name, the type/size/class of the vessel, the owner/customer for the vessel, the type of work done (new construction, overhaul, etc.), the date the vessel was delivered, and the fate or status of the vessel. For ships that remain in existence the current name is listed in the status/fate column; if no name is listed, the vessel retains its original name.

Some vessels built during this period were assigned hull numbers in the series used by General Dynamics Electric Boat Division, while others were assigned unique Quincy Shipbuilding Division hull numbers. The Electric Boat hull numbers are noted as "EB" in the list.

For conversions and reconditionings, the vessel's new name (at completion) is listed under "name", the original name and description are listed under "type", and the nature of the conversion is listed under "work type".

Fore River Shipyard Production Record

Hull	Name	Type/Descr.	Owner	Work Type	Delivered	Fate or Status
EB 160	*Greenling* (SSN 614)	*Permit* Class Attack Submarine (Incomplete)	Electric Boat Division for US Navy	Completion & Fitting Out	16 Nov 1967	Scrapped 1994
EB 162	*Gato* (SSN 615)	*Permit* Class Attack Submarine (Incomplete)	Electric Boat Division for US Navy	Completion & Fitting Out	25 Jan 1969	Scrapped 1996
EB	*Whale*	*Sturgeon* Class Attack	US Navy	New	27 Oct	Scrapped 1997

Fore River Shipyard Production Record, Part 3   Page 2 of 4

175	(SSN 638)	Submarine			1968	
EB 176	*Sunfish* (SSN 649)	*Sturgeon* Class Attack Submarine	US Navy	New	15 Mar 1969	Scrapped 1997
EB 177	*Vanguard* (T-AGM 19)	*Mission Buenaventura* Class Fleet Oiler *Mission San Fernando* (T-AO 122)	US Navy	Conversion to *Vanguard* Class Missile Range Instrumentation Ship	28 Feb 1966	Decom 1998; Pending Disposal
EB 178	*Redstone* (T-AGM 20)	*Mission Buenaventura* Class Fleet Oiler *Mission De Pala* (T-AO 114)	US Navy	Conversion to *Vanguard* Class Missile Range Instrumentation Ship	30 June 1966	Scrapped 1997
EB 179	*Mercury* (T-AGM 21)	*Mission Buenaventura* Class Fleet Oiler *Mission San Juan* (T-AO 126)	US Navy	Conversion to *Vanguard* Class Missile Range Instrumentation Ship	16 Sept 1966	Scrapped 1975
EB 183	--	Crew Boat	UAC	New	1966	Unknown
EB 184	*Kilauea* (AE 26)	*Kilauea* Class Ammunition Ship	US Navy	New	12 June 1968	In Service
EB 186	*L.Y. Spear* (AS 36)	*L.Y. Spear* Class Submarine Tender	US Navy	New	11 Feb 1970	Stricken 1999; Pending Disposal
EB 187	*Wichita* (AOR 1)	*Wichita* Class Replenishment Oiler	US Navy	New	9 May 1969	Stricken 1995; Pending Disposal
EB 188	*Butte* (AE 27)	*Kilauea* Class Ammunition Ship	US Navy	New	29 Nov 1968	In Service
EB 190	*Milwaukee* (AOR 2)	*Wichita* Class Replenishment Oiler	US Navy	New	3 Oct 1969	Stricken 1997; Pending Disposal
	Portland (LSD 37)	*Anchorage* Class Dock Landing Ship	US Navy	New	28 Aug 1970	In Service
	Pensacola (LSD 38)	*Anchorage* Class Dock Landing Ship	US Navy	New	16 Mar 1971	In Service (Taiwanese)
	Mount Vernon (LSD 39)	*Anchorage* Class Dock Landing Ship	US Navy	New	17 Apr 1972	In Service
	Dixon (AS 37)	*L.Y. Spear* Class Submarine Tender	US Navy	New	7 May 1971	Stricken 1995; Pending Disposal
	Kansas City (AOR 3)	*Wichita* Class Replenishment Oiler	US Navy	New	1 May 1970	Stricken 1997; Pending Disposal
	Savannah (AOR 4)	*Wichita* Class Replenishment Oiler	US Navy	New	28 Oct 1970	Stricken 1998; Pending Disposal
	Fort Fisher (LSD 40)	*Anchorage* Class Dock Landing Ship	US Navy	New	8 Nov 1972	Stricken 1998; Pending

Fore River Shipyard Production Record, Part 3   Page 3 of 4

						Disposal
	Wabash (AOR 5)	Wichita Class Replenishment Oiler	US Navy	New	21 Oct 1971	Stricken 1997; Pending Disposal
	Kalamazoo (AOR 6)	Wichita Class Replenishment Oiler	US Navy	New	10 July 1973	Stricken 1998; Pending Disposal
	Doctor Lykes	873' SeaBee Barge Carrier	Lykes Brothers Steamship Co.	New	21 June 1972	In Reserve (Cape Mendocino)
	Almeria Lykes	873' SeaBee Barge Carrier	Lykes Brothers Steamship Co.	New	26 Sept 1972	In Reserve (Cape May
	Tillie Lykes	873' SeaBee Barge Carrier	Lykes Brothers Steamship Co.	New	16 Mar 1973	In Reserve (Cape Mohican)
41	LNG Aquarius	936' LNG Tanker	Wilmington Trust Co.	New	7 June 1977	In Service
42	LNG Aries	936' LNG Tanker	Wilmington Trust Co.	New	13 Dec 1977	In Service
44	LNG Gemini	936' LNG Tanker	Cherokee	New	7 Sept 1978	In Service
46	LNG Capricorn	936' LNG Tanker	Wilmington Trust Co.	New	22 June 1978	In Service
47	LNG Leo	936' LNG Tanker	Cherokee	New	7 Dec 1978	In Service
48	LNG Taurus	936' LNG Tanker	Cherokee	New	7 Aug 1979	In Service
49	LNG Virgo	936' LNG Tanker	Cherokee	New	7 Dec 1979	In Service
50	LNG Libra	936' LNG Tanker	Cherokee	New	12 Apr 1979	In Service
53	Lake Charles	936' LNG Tanker	Lachmar, Inc.	New	15 May 1980	In Service
54	Louisiana	936' LNG Tanker	Lachmar, Inc.	New	25 Sept 1980	In Service
55	Bulkfleet Pennsylvania	24,400 DWT, 502' Tank Barge	Bulkfleet Marine Corp.	New	5 Feb 1981	Unknown
56	Bulkfleet Texas	24,400 DWT, 502' Tank Barge	Bulkfleet Marine Corp.	New	Unk.	Unknown
73		20,000 DWT, 471' Tank Barge	Coastwise Trading Co.	New	Unk.	Unknown
74		20,000 DWT, 471' Tank Barge	Coastwise Trading Co.	New	Unk.	Unknown
75		20,000 DWT, 415' Tank Barge	Coastwise Trading Co.	New	Unk.	Unknown
82		20,000 DWT, 471' Chemical Tank Barge	Coastwise Trading Co.	New	Unk.	Unknown
	Overseas	123,000 DWT Tanker	Unknown	Repairs &	7 Feb 1981	In Service

Fore River Shipyard Production Record, Part 3   Page 4 of 4

		Boston			Modification		
		Neptune (T-ARC 2)	*Neptune* Class Cable Ship	US Navy	Reconstruction	8 Oct 1982	Stricken 1992; Pending Disposal
		Charles Carrol	Waterman Corp.	695' Roll-on/Roll-off Freighter	New	15 Apr 1982	In Service (*MAJ Stephen W. Pless*)
		Energy Independence	686' Collier	New England Collier Co.	New	6 Aug 1983	In Service (*Energy Enterprise*)
		Sea-Shuttle	Unknown	Unknown	New?	1 Nov 1983	Unknown
	61	*2nd Lt John P. Bobo*	673' C8-M-MA134j Maritime Prepositioning Ship	AMSEA for USN/MSC	New	14 Feb 1985	In Service
	62	*PFC Dewayne T Williams*	673' C8-M-MA134j Maritime Prepositioning Ship	AMSEA for USN/MSC	New	6 June 1985	In Service
	63	*1st Lt Baldomero Lopez*	673' C8-M-MA134j Maritime Prepositioning Ship	AMSEA for USN/MSC	New	20 Nov 1985	In Service
	64	*1st Lt Jack Lummus*	673' C8-M-MA134j Maritime Prepositioning Ship	AMSEA for USN/MSC	New	6 Mar 1986	In Service
	65	*SGT William R. Button*	673' C8-M-MA134j Maritime Prepositioning Ship	AMSEA for USN/MSC	New	22 May 1986	In Service

Major Sources:
List of Ships Built at the Quincy Yard. Central Technical Department of Bethlehem Steel Company, Shipbuilding Division, Quincy, MA., with unofficial addenda.

Dictionary of American Naval Fighting Ships. Naval Historical Center, Washington, D.C., 1959-1991.

Special thanks to everyone who has provided updated information about these ships.

▌▐ ☰ ▬ ■ ◆ ⫼ ▐ ▌ ● ▭ ▌ ◢ ⊠ ⊗ ◥ ◻ ▭ ▐ ▆ ▬ ▐ ▌ ◥ ⤬ ◳ ✚ ▨ ◣

Back to the *Hazegray* Shipbuilding Pages

SENATOR TED KENNEDY SAID, "MY FATHER WORKED HERE.

The Fore River Shipyard will once again be a symbol of our leadership. And I will do all I can to insure that this leadership continues to thrive. The shipbuilding industry has been struggling in this country as a whole. Employment has dropped to a 40 year low. American-built ships carry less than one percent of world trade. That is unacceptable."

Senator John McCain said, "We have an obligation to protect the taxpayers' dollars by ensuring that this is a viable project. It is my desire that the Quincy shipyard, into which the state of Massachusetts and the city of Quincy have invested significant resources, will be a successful venture."

President Clinton said about shipbuilding and the Quincy yard in particular, "Shipbuilding is one of the keys to America's national defense and helping our shipbuilders succeed commercially is an important goal of defense conversion."

"This administration is committed to preserving highly skilled American jobs and we believe that American shipbuilding can compete and win in world markets."

What happened...? SHIPBUILDING USED TO BE ONE OF THE TOP FIVE INDUSTRIES IN THE U.S.A.

0-595-27532-X